The Weekend Crafter®

Making
Books & Journals

the
Weekend
Crafter®

Making Books & Journals

20 Great Weekend Projects

CONSTANCE E. RICHARDS

LARK
BOOKS

A Division of Sterling
Publishing Co., Inc.
New York

ART DIRECTOR & PRODUCTION:
CELIA NARANJO

PHOTOGRAPHY:
EVAN BRACKEN

ILLUSTRATIONS:
GWEN DIEHN

PRODUCTION ASSISTANCE:
HANNES CHAREN

EDITORIAL ASSISTANCE:
HEATHER SMITH

Library of Congress Cataloging-in-Publishing Data
Richards, Constance E.
    Making books & journals : 20 great weekend projects / Constance
E. Richards.
        p. cm—(The weekend crafter)
    Includes index.
    ISBN 1-57990-092-5 (paper)
    1. Bookbinding. I. Title. II. Series.
Z271.R514 1999   98-45006
686.3 —dc21   CIP

10 9 8 7 6

Published by Lark Books, a division of
Sterling Publishing Co., Inc.
387 Park Avenue South, New York, N.Y. 10016

© 2000, Lark Books

Distributed in Canada by Sterling Publishing,
c/o Canadian Manda Group, One Atlantic Ave., Suite 105
Toronto, Ontario, Canada M6K 3E7

Distributed in Australia by Capricorn Link (Australia) Pty Ltd.
P.O. Box 704, Windsor, NSW 2756 Australia

Distributed in the U.K. by:
Guild of Master Craftsman Publications Ltd.
Castle Place 166 High Street, Lewes, East Sussex, England, BN7 1XU
Tel: (+ 44) 1273 477374 Fax: (+ 44) 1273 478606
Email: pubs@thegmcgroup.com Web: www.gmcpublications.com

If you have questions or comments about this book, please contact:
Lark Books, 67 Broadway, Asheville, NC 28801, (828) 253-0467

Printed in China

ISBN 1-57990-092-5

CONTENTS

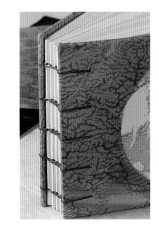

INTRODUCTION

Not only can the contents of books magically transport a person to other worlds, but we like to think the structure of the books themselves can, too. Rather than picturing a book as paper between two covers, think: pop-up, fold-out, opening like a blossom, dangling baubles, trinkets, woven threads, fruit that opens up, secret pockets, bejeweled, rolled-up and tucked-away...books for all occasions, all steps of life! This exciting menagerie of ideas and tangible results, doable in a single weekend, are what we would like to introduce to you with this book.

Beginning with scrolls and tablets, bookmaking dates back to before the fourth century. Bookbinding techniques evolved thereafter in ancient Egypt and continued through the ages, spanning continents and layers of society, as a high art form, and now—as a science—in book preservation.

Bookmaking as a hobby has seen an upsurge of popularity. Perhaps as we come to the end of our own century, our quest for simple beauty, once again made by our own hands, deepens.

With this book, we don't expect you to become a bookmaker overnight; however, it should help you along in generating ideas, creating inspiration, teaching you the very basics, and allowing your imagination to run wild.

Starting out, you need not use the most expensive handmade paper, nor accumulate the most up-to-date tools or equipment for your weekend endeavors. We do urge you to practice a few basic elements of bookmaking and to choose your supplies wisely, which will always assure your books maintain a high quality and can be preserved for years to come.

Eleven exceptional designers from around the country have created the pieces which appear in this book. Our artists are a conglomeration of professional bookmakers, skilled crafters, talented hobbyists, and even some beginners who just had to scratch their creative itch! Many of the books in our gallery sections have been on display in museums and galleries. Some even fetch a pretty price. Others were made as thank-yous and gifts for friends. A couple were even made during a beginner's bookmaking class. As you can see...the sky is the limit.

We have chosen a variety of bookmaking formats for you to try, including accordion folding, coptic binding, stab-binding, hexagonal folding, and many others. If you are not familiar with these terms, you soon will be! We use a variety of bindings, including such non-traditional materials as wire. Some of our books use no stitching at all, requiring only a simple folding method. Some of them fold with secret compartments, some of them can be used as jewelry, others as ornaments. We provide both large and miniature formats.

Certain books contain interesting stamps or decorative painting techniques. We give you the basic format for making the book, but generally leave the choice of stamping—what kind, how many, where—-up to you. Follow your own creative notions, using our offerings as examples of one version of the book you may like to make. We do discuss painting and collage techniques in a few of the projects, which feature these kinds of ornamentation, but again, colors and design are what will make the books you decide upon uniquely yours.

We have modified some of the designers' instructions to fit our special step-by-step photo format, and think you will enjoy the simplicity with which you can craft some of these projects in just a few hours, or over a weekend. Once you learn the basic folding, sewing and gluing techniques, you will work much faster and more effeciently than at the beginning. If you have taken bookmaking classes before, or are an advanced bookmaker, we are sure you will find some interesting ideas in this book as well. The artists we queried have developed their own fascinating designs, some of which are first-time inventions. And many of the pieces are so simply explained that they make great activities to do with children.

There's no excuse not to try one of these projects. The old argument of not enough time, won't cut it. These can even be made in front of the television, as a Saturday-morning meditational excercise, or as a party theme. Try a "Making Our Own Baby-Album" baby shower. Or a bridal shower where the guests each make one page to go into the hand-made wedding album. Kids love taking their finished books home as party favors from a birthday bash, and who's to say a future groom wouldn't mind his last days of bachelorhood forever archived in a scrapbook made by his friends? A thank-you book says a lot more than a thank-you note, and a little book of hand-drawn poems and sketches can certainly ignite a new romance. In this world of disposable everything, buy-it-anywhere—a weekend spent making gifts by hand, for yourself or for others, is time well-spent and well-appreciated.

We also issue a warning: book-making can be addictive! While piecing together the various steps for photographing, editor, photographer, and model became so enthralled that we often finished making our own little version of the books right then and there. Then we went home, and made more.

Most of all, enjoy experimenting with the books we demonstrate here. Follow our instructions word-for-word, or feel free to deviate and improvise. It's really up to you. We hope you have as much fun as we did.

Gwen Diehn's "Lettuces" book opens to the left, the right, up, down, inside and out, with little arrows for guides. Inside the pockets on the back of each page are seeds corresponding to the plants indicated on the front—another ingenious gathering of text and pages, culminating in a "book" and giving credence to the concept that a book comes in many shapes, sizes and forms.

GETTING STARTED

Getting started in bookmaking requires precious few specialized tools, if any. In fact, you can start today, without even going shopping. All you need is paper, glue, thread, a needle, and some cardboard. Decorative items for your book cover can be found all over your home—buttons, earrings, ribbon, paint, ink, pressed flowers or leaves, lace, wax, paper doilies, wire, charms, sand...set your imagination free.

Once you have learned the basic techniques, chances are you'd like to try your hand at a few of these books in earnest. All of your tools and materials may be found in art supply shops. You can also find many of the components, such as craft glue, tape, hole punchers, needles, paper clips, clamps, drills, cardboard, scissors, and an assortment of matte knives and craft knives in regular mass market stores or hardware stores.

Undoubtedly, one of the most thrilling parts of making books is choosing your paper. For this purchase, the art supply store is truly the best option. A myriad of paper in varying colors, textures, and thicknesses has become available at non-prohibitive prices. Choose from banana leaf, kozo fiber, petal-infused, Japanese rice paper, and the list goes on. Some are reversible, so a different color will show depending on the way you have folded your book. Some bookmakers even make their own paper (but that's a subject for another Weekend Crafter).

The more books you make, the more your own style will show through, be it a particular motif, color scheme, decoration, etc. Eventually, you may even invent your own particular book format. To assist in recreating the books we demonstrate here, full-color photos accompanied by step-by-step instructions lead your way for each project. We have provided patterns for making templates in the back of the book for several of the projects which feature a particular design or decorative motif. You may copy them, enlarge or minimize them, and transfer them onto your project.

Tools

You will need a few, but not all of the following tools to begin your odyssey into bookmaking. Read through the supplies-and-tools part of each project you are interested in making, and invest only in the tools you will need. If you only plan on making small books which fold, or are sewn with a needle, then you have no use for a hand drill, or hole puncher, for example. Eventually, you may want to increase the contents of your tool chest, but at your own pace.

- Awl
- Scoring tool (bone folder, or large paper clips)
- Clamps or clothespins
- Ruler, square-angle rule
- Craft needles (straight and curved)
- Pencil
- Hole punch
- Hand drill
- Glue brush
- Scissors
- Matte knife
- Craft knife

Supplies

PAPER

Paper is the integral part of your book—it makes up the pages and covers the boards which will protect the inside pages. For the the text pages, a good quality copy paper, heavy writing paper, watercolor paper, or linen paper will work well. Handmade paper is another option. For the endpapers and exterior of the cover, you will most likely choose a decorative paper with some texture and color.

When preparing to cut the paper you will be using for the book, you must first make note of the grain. The grain is the direction the fibers run in a sheet of paper. It usually should run parallel to the spine of your book. If you can't see the way the grain is arranged in a piece of paper, you can test it yourself by bending the paper from side to side, or from top to bottom. Whichever way it bends more easily is the direction the grain runs. If you feel resistance, or if the paper cracks where you have folded it, this means the grain runs in the opposite direction. Take note, however: In handmade paper the fibers mesh in a helter-skelter fashion, and the grain does not run in one particular direction. You will have to watch our for the grain in machine-made papers.

All grains should run parallel to the spine in a book, and they should be aligned to each other.

Clockwise from bottom left: hand drill, pencil, awls and needle tool, bone folders, waxed thread, straight and curved sewing needles, straight-edge, C-clamps, metal clips, hole punch, scissors, craft knife, matte knife, clothespins, glue brush, square-angle rule, matte board. Center: glue

Gwen Diehn created this one-of-a-kind artist's book with illustration, wood block prints, calligraphied text, metallic paints, and watercolor. "Hours for the Beach" opens like a regular book but expands out into a star-book, because of its flexible spine.

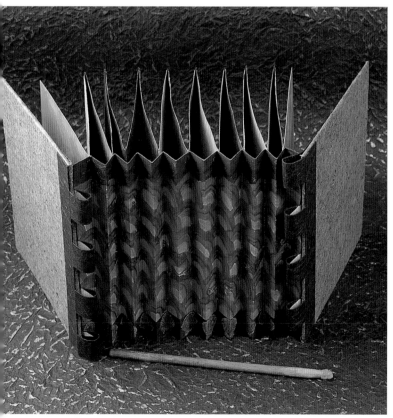

Pull out the wooden stick supporting the spine of this book and it opens into an accordion of painted details.

Whenever gluing together paper, *signatures* (several pages nestled within each other, creating an interior text section of the book), and cover board, always remember that anything supporting another material needs to be heavier than what it supports. This also means the cover of the book must be heavier than the paper inside, or else the weight of the papers which are supposedly being supported will tear from the "support".

CLOTH

Cloth makes an excellent book cover. It's easy to fold, is durable, and makes for good texture. Special book cloth, however, is expensive. It is a strongly-woven cotton or linen, and is specially treated with a starch filler to prevent glue from filtering through the weave of the cloth. Sometimes it has a tissue or paper lining.

You can make your own sturdy book cloth, however, by spraying the material with cloth guard or an acrylic gilt medium, coating only the back.

THREAD

Always use waxed thread. You can wax your own thread by gently running it through a small pot of beeswax (found at craft stores). This ensures that the thread will not wear thin and eventually break at the spine with continuous opening and closing of the book. Linen thread is the most durable, but again, the most expensive. Any strong thread will do, such as upholsterer's thread, buttonhole, or carpet thread. You will not want your thread to be stretchy, which can ruin your entire project if the thread stretches out of shape after it has been sewn.

More often than not, the thread will be seen on the cover or the spine of your book, so you may want to use decorative and colorful threads, or even ribbon, cord, or strong decorative beading or sewing threads.

ADHESIVES

Pastes and glues are what will hold the cover paper on your book cover, the endpapers on the inside covers, and the decorative bits in or on your book. Some bookmakers prefer to make their own paste from wheat or rice starch. For a weekend project, we recommend buying craft glue. PVA, or polyvinyl acetate, is the most common and can be found in craft shops and mass market stores.

Glue sticks are tricky. They are quick and easy to use, but they can be awkward for large surfaces, and dry very quickly. It's better to stay away from them altogether. If you must use them, look carefully at the label to see which ones are archival, or non-acidic.

Use a glue brush for distributing the glue properly and evenly. Always be sure to work your glue *into* the paper, rather than just spreading it around on top. To do this, hold the glue brush in your fist and bear down, working the glue into the fibers of the paper or boards in your project.

Keep waxed paper near your work area and use it to protect the other pages and materials from the gluing going on. Use the waxed paper, also, for wrapping the book when placing it in a press or under heavy books.

Scrap paper is also a must with its many uses—creating a barrier to protect your work surface while gluing or cutting, for *burnishing,* or smoothing out the paper over just-glued surfaces.

Working with glue and paint can create spills and smudges, so always keep one wet and one dry cloth near your work area.

When gluing paper and board together, as a general rule, the glue should be put on the paper, and the board positioned onto the paper. Especially if the paper is thick, the glue-dampened paper will more easily bend around the board's edge. With very thin paper, and cloth, you may coat the board with glue, as the adhesive might seep through the thin material. In several of our step-by-step shots, we have shown brushing glue onto the board.

PRESERVING PAPER, GLUE, AND THREAD

Archival, acid-free material is an absolute must, unless you plan for your hard-wrought work to fall apart in a few weeks. If using ink, avoid ball-point pens. They are acidic and will stain the paper. A waterproof, fine-line pen is what you can use instead.

For covers, avoid soft cardboard, chip board, or anything other than acid-free matte board. Avoid wood pulp paper. Rag paper is better. Construction paper will fade and rot. Instead, use colored copy paper or craft paper.

THE BASICS

Making Covers, Corners, and Cover Treatments

Obviously one of the most impressive and important parts of your book will be its cover. To ensure that the cover is creaseless, won't buckle, and will stand up to repeated handling and opening of the book, learn the basic elements of the proper way to cover your book.

Here, we use three simple ways of attaching the cover paper to the cover board. If the directions do not tell you, leave approximately an extra inch of cover paper around the four sides of your cover board.

1) For thinner paper and cloth, fold the corner of the paper down over the cover board and glue. You may want to snip off the very tip of the paper corner. Fold one side over the glued piece and crease with your bone folder, glue 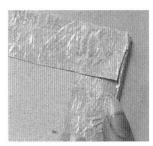 this side down over the top of the corner you have just glued, and onto the board. Do the same with the adjacent side.

2) For average to thick paper, cut off the corners of your material at a diagonal fold and glue one side of the paper down onto the board. Part of the paper will overlap the adjacent side of paper. Press the paper down at a slight angle over the yet-to-be-glued paper. Fold and glue the adjacent corner over the already glued corner and board.

3) For cloth and paper, cut a small square over the corners of the board, then fold and glue the flaps of the paper or cloth down towards the inside of the board.

Using one of the covering procedures, give the cover a fine finish by *burnishing*, or flattening, the paper in order for it to be completely smooth, free of creases, and fitting snugly up against the cover board. This can be done with a bone-folder (a specialized tool made from animal bone),

Kristin Cozzolino's "Sand" is covered with a thick mixture of sand and adhesive. The paper's edges are deckeled.

Julia Monroe's "Sewing Journal" was made entirely on a sewing machine.

or the back of a spoon. After gluing the cover paper down, but before gluing the flaps, turn the book over, place waxed or scrap paper over the cover, and bear down on your implement moving it in circular motions over the entire surface. This will force out any air bubbles or spaces caught between the paper and glue, giving the cover a smooth surface. Glue the flaps and burnish those. You may choose to burnish the front once again.

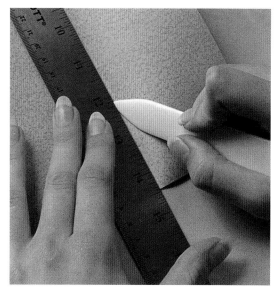

Whenever making folds or creases in your bookmaking process, score the paper first. With your scoring tool—the bone folder or blunt edge of a paper clip—bear down on the paper you intend to crease or fold and pull the tool toward you along the side of a ruler, to ensure a straight line. Score at least four times for a smooth and permanent crease.

When making holes in the cover board, or the signatures, make the smallest hole possible with an awl, needle, or hole puncher and use the smallest sized needle possible for pulling the thread through, since the holes will most likely enlarge anyway with repeated opening and closing.

Finally, to preserve your book, treat the cover. You can paint an acrylic medium over the cover to give it a shiny finish, which secures it against destructive skin oils from fingerprints, against dirt, and against scratches. You can instead choose to give your book a wax finish by polishing the cover paper with wax and buff-

ing it with a soft cloth. Let it dry overnight. For cloth, spray the cover with a guard before you put the cover and the signatures together.

As a final touch, you may also want to burnish the cover all over to smooth the surface of the paper and bring a slight sheen to it, depending on the paper you have used. Textured paper should be left alone, but fairly thin or not overly textured paper will work fine. Simply burnish with a bone folder, as instructed above, over the entire surface of the cover.

Decorating the cover is an individual decision. You may like the simple lines and planes of your paper. You may want to adhere various small baubles to the front cover. You may choose to paint it, or glue a collage onto it. Stamping is also a nice option. Adhering other bits and pieces of decorative paper to the cover is also attractive. We offer several of these variations in this book.

When to decorate is another decision left up to you. Some designers like to adorn the cover before sewing. Others prefer to leave this to the last, lest something be knocked off in the sewing or binding process. Generally, any decoration which is not flat, has a special texture which could be compressed, or is very delicate, should be left to the very end. Paintings, sketches, or stamping can be done to the cover before it is bound.

Gwen Diehn's "Granitus" displays the use of bone clasps holding together hinges and wood as the cover boards.

Handmade paper is used for the text pages and an inscription in wax decorates the inside cover.

Folded Book with Pockets

DESIGN: **BETH WEISS**

Assembled by strategic folding, this book needs no glue or thread to hold it together. It's easy to learn and a wonderful first project for kids.

YOU WILL NEED

Decorative paper of any light to medium weight,
35 x 4¼ inches (89.5 x 11 cm)

Text-weight paper

2 squares of cover board

Craft knife

Ruler

Scoring tool (bone folder or other tool to press folds flat)

TIP: A plastic floor mat (usually used under chairs) makes a suitable cutting surface for papers too long to fit on a desk top cutting mat.

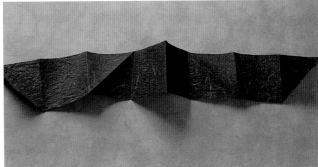

1 Fold the strip into an accordion of eight panels. Crease the indicated panels diagonally according to the photo. Flatten all creases with the bone folder.

2 Fold the center diagonals down and behind.

VARIATIONS

This cover is a wonderful way to use exotic papers that may be too thin, transparent, or textured for gluing. The repeated folding makes them sturdy enough for use as a cover. Many handmade imported papers come in large sheets that make it possible to cut one long strip.

For making other sizes, just remember to cut the decorative paper in proportion of eight squares long by less than one square wide. When using a two-toned reversible paper, experiment with folding the final flaps back rather than down so that both colors are visible.

3 Fold the sides in toward the center.

4 Fold the tails behind and up.

5 Fold the end corners down.

6 Fold the flaps down and tuck them in.

7 If a stiffer cover is desired, insert squares of index card or book board, cut slightly smaller than the book.

8 Slide the outer pages of a square page accordion or other text block into center openings inside cover.

Roll-Up Travel Journal

DESIGN: **GWEN DIEHN**

Ingenious in its simplicity, the Roll-Up Travel Journal comes with its own protective case. Throw it in your backpack or beachbag when finished writing or sketching and the tube protects your journal from being crushed or dog-eared.

1 Turn the corrugated paper so that one of its short ends faces you. Roll up the paper, beginning at the 5-inch end that is nearest you. As it rolls, the paper will bend between the ribs. Keep rolling until you have a fat roll of paper five inches tall. Unroll the paper. It will stay bent and curly, but it will have enough stability from the ribs that it will provide a support upon which you can draw or write. Fold the paper in half.

YOU WILL NEED

A single thickness of corrugated cardboard paper (available in art supply or specialty paper stores), 5 x 11 inches (13 x 28 cm)

Decorative paper, 5 x 11 inches

10 to 12 sheets of drawing or writing paper, 5 x 10 inches (13 x 25.5 cm)

2 feet (61.5 cm) of heavy waxed thread

Cardboard tube, such as the tube from a roll of paper towels

Corrugated cardboard paper, approximately 5 x 8 inches (13 x 20.5 cm) for the tube

Craft glue

Awl

Needle

Scissors

Metal ruler

Pencil

Craft knife

Glue brush

VARIATION

You can also tie a thick, pretty cord around the tube lengthwise (bringing it through the tube itself) and tie it to your belt loop. Just pop the journal out of its case when you see something to sketch or write about on your travels, pop it back in when you are finished, and you're ready to go.

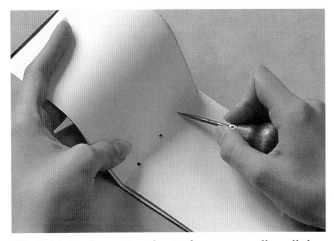

2 Fold the decorative sheet of paper as well as all the sheets of writing paper in half and slip them inside the cardboard cover. The decorated side of the top sheet should face up. Unfold the book to the center page. Use an awl to poke three holes through the cover and all the sheets of paper at once, about one inch apart, in the fold of the book. Be careful to keep the pages still, as the holes must stay lined up. Gently wiggle the awl to enlarge the holes until they are big enough for a needle to fit through.

3 Thread needle with heavy thread. Don't tie a knot. Poke needle through center hole from outside of book. Pull through, leaving a 3-or 4-inch (7.5 or 10 cm) tail on the outside. From the inside, poke needle through either one of the other holes, and pull thread through tightly, being careful to leave tail hanging out. From the outside, while holding onto the tail, poke needle back into center hole. Pull thread through to the inside of the book, still holding onto tail. Poke needle into remaining hole from the inside. Pull thread tightly, and tie it on the outside to the tail. Tie as closely as possible to center hole. Double knot, and trim ends.

4 On the front cover, lightly draw the shape that you want to cut out. A ruler may be useful, but you could also draw freehand, depending on the design. Then open the book so that the front cover is on the right and all the rest of the book is on the left. Place the book opened this way on a scrap piece of cardboard or cutting surface. Use the craft knife to cut out the shape you have drawn. When you close the book, the decorative paper should show through the shape you have cut out of the cover.

5 To make the case, cut the cardboard tube the same height as the height of the book. Cut a piece of corrugated paper the height of the tube by approximately 8 inches (20.5 cm). Make the piece long enough to wrap around the tube with a half-inch (1.5 cm) overlap. Glue the paper to the outside of the tube. Press firmly to help the paper adhere to the tube. When the tube is dry, roll up the book and slip it into the tube. The tube fits easily in your pocket or a book bag, making it easy to carry the journal with you.

Mailable Journal

DESIGN: **STEPHANIE ELLIS**

A delightfully simple booklet to make, the Mailable Journal is a letter and envelope in one. Use more pages to compose a journal to keep for yourself, or mail the decorated creation off to a friend.

1 Using the decorative paper, make a fold at 4 inches (10 cm) and fold again at 4¼ inches (11 cm). At the 2¾-inch (7 cm) end of the sheet, measure 1¼ inches (3.5 cm) on each side and mark with a pencil. Make a cut in a straight line from the pencil mark to the edge of the fold. Fold the paper you have just cut to form an envelope.

2 Measure 2½ (6.5 cm) inches from the bottom of the envelope to the edge of the fold-over flap and make two small pencil marks on either side of the flap. Using a straight edge or ruler, make a cut between the two pencil marks.

Insert the folded piece of writing paper and center it between the edges of the envelope. There should be about ⅛ inch (5 mm) on each side.

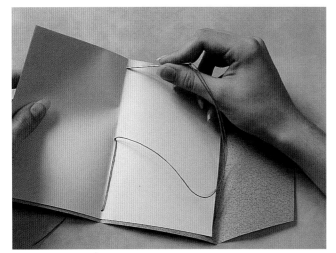

3 With the needle, gently poke three holes, one in the center of the crease and two ¼ inch (1 cm) from the edges of the writing paper. With the thread in the needle, insert the needle into the center hole, come through a side hole, reenter the center hole, and bring the needle back through the other side hole.

4 Tie a small knot at the center opening. Tie off the ends of the thread. You may choose to decorate the thread with beads, paper cut-outs or other objects before the last step. Cut pieces of decorative paper and glue them to the outside of the envelope. Fold the booklet together and insert the flap into the slit you have made.

Lotus Map Book

DESIGN: **GWEN DIEHN**

The Lotus Map Book opens like the petals of a flower, revealing its contents. The book may hold a collection of poems, recipes, or pressed flowers. As you turn the pages, each part of the collection will burst forth center stage.

1 Square each sheet of paper by folding it diagonally. Cut off the leftover piece across the bottom of the triangle. Unfold the paper, and there will be a square with a crease going from one corner to the other. Fold the paper square back along the crease and press the fold with your finger to make it sharp. Unfold paper and fold it sharply in half from top to bottom. Keeping paper folded, fold it in half the other way, pressing creases each time. When unfolded, the paper will have three creases. Fold again along the diagonal (corner to corner), but this time the opposite way. Pinch the sides of the diagonal creases so that the plain two boxes fold up and toward each other. Repeat this step for each sheet of paper.

2 To attach the pages to each other, place a folded piece of paper on the table in front of you in a diamond position. Keep the two folded edges to your left and the unfolded edges to your right. Slip a piece of waxed paper underneath the top sheet of the diamond to protect the paper underneath. Brush glue over the entire top sheet of the diamond. Place another diamond exactly on top of the first one, with edges in the same position. Press down to glue the sheets together and repeat with all sheets.

YOU WILL NEED

Old map, cut in sections measuring 8½ x 11 inches (20 x 28 cm)

2 pieces of chip board or cover board, 4½ inches (11.5 cm) square

2 sheets of decorated cover paper, 6 inches (15 cm) square

Craft glue

Waxed paper

2 feet (62 cm) of ribbon, ⅛ to ¼ inch wide (5 mm to 1 cm)

Scissors

Glue brush

Pencil

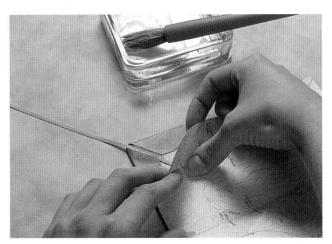

3 Cover the two pieces of cardboard, placing one in the center of a piece of decorative paper. Draw its outline, then draw glue tabs one inch out from each edge. Use a square cut into the paper at each corner, still keeping the square of paper attached. Lightly score the inside edges of the flaps if the paper is thick.

5 Place the two covers, outside down, with two of their corners ½ inch (1.5 cm) apart, for closing. Put a strip of glue from corner to corner across the two covers. Place the ribbon across the strip of glue. Slip waxed paper underneath the top diamond of the pile of glued paper. Spread glue all over the top sheet and press it against the inside front cover. The ribbon will be sandwiched between the cover and the pages. Repeat with the back cover.

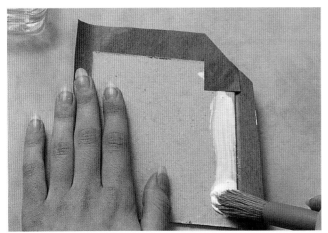

4 Put glue over the entire inside of the piece of paper and replace the cover board. You may put glue on the board at the side of the tabs, first gluing down the small square, then the side flaps over that. Press down all over both sides of the cover so that the paper is glued flat with no bubbles. Repeat for the other cover.

6 You may add a decorative title to the front cover. Here, decorative paper is stamped and glued in the center. Tie the ribbon.

Dos-à-Dos Sketch Journal

DESIGN: **GWEN DIEHN**

The French title of this journal denotes not only its structure, but also its unique style. Each section acts like an individual book, and can be used for separate subjects.

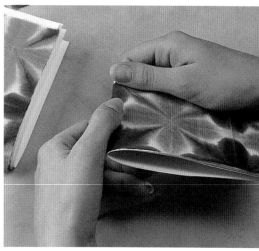

1 Make two stacks, each having a piece of decorative paper on top of six to eight sheets of writing or drawing paper. Fold all pages in half sideways. Crease them firmly to make two booklets, or signatures.

YOU WILL NEED

6-8 sheets of writing or drawing paper for each section of the book (each sheet should be wide enough to fold in half, making two sheets in one)

2 sheets of decorative paper, the same size as the writing or drawing paper

Cover paper (same height as text pages, and as wide as 3 text pages)

4 feet (1.24 m) of waxed thread

Beads to decorate binding (optional)

Scoring tool (bone folder, paper clips)

Large paper clips

Straight needle

Scissors

Hole punch

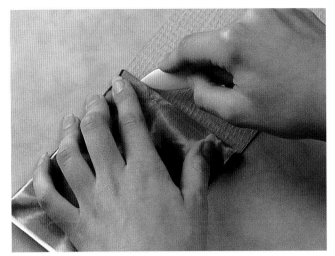

2 Lay a signature on top of the cover sheet at the left end. Mark by scoring with the bone folder along the right edge of the signature. Move the signature so it lines up along the first line scored and score another line at the right edge of the signature. Repeat the step, and be sure each section is the same size. Fold cover on first score line, turn cover sheet over and fold it on next scored line. It should look like the letter "Z" from the side.

3 Slip a signature into the first fold. Open the book and place it on a protected surface, such as cardboard. Paperclip the signature to the cover so that the crease of the signature is nested inside the crease of the cover. Use an awl to poke a hole in the center of the crease. Poke another hole midway between the top of the crease and the first hole. Poke a third hole midway between the bottom and the top of the crease and the middle hole.

4 Push the needle from the outside of the cover through the middle hole of one of the signatures and the cover. Pull the thread until a tail of 5 inches (13 cm) is left. Slip the tail under one of the paperclips to hold it in place. Poke the needle into the top hole and pull the thread firmly. Bring the needle out of the top hole, cross over the middle hole, and poke into the bottom hole. Pull needle back through the middle hole.

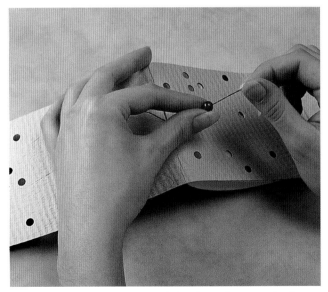

5 Tie the tail to the end of the thread across the long stitch, slipping a bead onto one end before you tie it. Repeat these steps for the remaining signatures. You may punch holes or cut shapes into the covers before or after sewing so that the decorative paper shows through.

Fencerow Manifesto, Gwen Diehn with Amy Turkle

In Place, Gwen Diehn

Sand Bottom Journal, Gwen Diehn

Ocean Book, *Kristin Cozzolino*

Things are Not as They Seem, Nor Are They Otherwise, *Gwen Diehn*

Saturnalia, *Gwen Diehn*

Rows of Oats, *Kristin Cozzolino*

Enchanted, *Joyce Brodsky*

Granitus, *Gwen Diehn*

Jelly Bean Books

DESIGN: **PAULA BEARDELL KRIEG**

Called so because of their relatively small size and colorful covers, these little Jelly Bean Books can be decorated with any number of beads, threads, pressed flowers, and other tidbits.

1 To make a template: On 14 x 8½ inch paper draw a 9½ x 2-inch (24.5 x 5 cm) rectangle. Mark through rectangle vertically with lines 5 inches (13 cm) long at 2½ inches (6.5 cm), 5 inches, and 7¼ inches (18.5 cm). These mark the placement for the fold lines. (The original rectangle is now divided into four rectangles that are 2½ inches wide, 2½ inches wide, 2¼ inches (6 cm) wide, and 2¼ inches wide.) Your template is now ready for step 2.

YOU WILL NEED

Scrap paper, 14 x 8½ inches (30.5 x 18 cm) for template piece

6 strips of writing or drawing paper, 4¾ x 2 inches (12.5 x 5 cm)

Medium-weight paper, 9½ x 2 inches (24.5 x 5 cm)

Heavy thread, such as embroidery thread or waxed linen thread

Decorative add-ons for the cover, such as stickers, cut-outs from greeting cards, beads, colored papers, and pressed flowers

Ruler

Pencil

Scoring tool (bone folder, paper clips)

Craft glue

Glue brush

Scissors

Craft knife

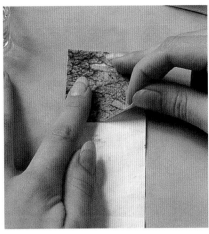 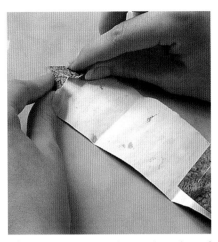 

2 Lay a strip of 9½ x 2-inch paper on the 9½ x 2-inch template rectangle. Mark the fold lines on the strip, score, and fold. Reopen. Apply glue to the two 2¼-inch sections. Glue these sections together.

3 Create a triangle on the edge of the first 2½-inch section by folding in right triangles from the corners. Glue down the triangles.

4 Fold six sheets of 4¾ x 2-inch paper in half, one at a time. Nest the papers together. This is a single signature, and it is the book block. Align the spine of the signature with the first fold (the fold closest to the edge, which is now triangular). With the book closed, make marks on either side of the flap ⅝ inch (1.7 cm) from the edges of the triangular flap.

Guarding the pages beneath, cut through the lower flap, making a slit which joins the two marks. Tuck the triangular edge into the slit.

5 Snip off the corners of the spine of the book. Open the book to the middle of the signature. Wrap heavy thread or cord around the inner fold to the outside, securing the signature to the cover. Tie a knot. Add beads or other decoration.

6 Close the book, first folding down the doubled 2½-inch section on top of the signature, then laying the triangular-shaped section down over the doubled section. Tuck triangle into slit to close.

Note: Creating a template will ease your work with making future Jelly Bean Books. You won't have to remeasure the basic design.

Angel Photo Album

DESIGN: **DAISY KAPPEN**

This personalized memory album is one of the simplest and most satisfying books to make, because it will be pulled out for family and friends again and again. Design a cover to reflect your personal style with themes of animals, flowers, folk patterns, etc.

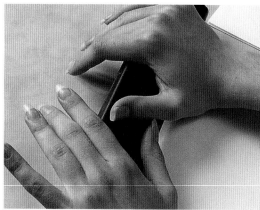

1 For the album pages, cut 20 8 x 10-inch squares of cream heavyweight paper and punch holes at the top center. Punch holes into the two squares of matte board.

TIP: For the decorative cover of this album, the designer made a 3-D angel (see template in back of book), whose cut-out components she stacked, beginning with the backing paper, doily, dress, doll face, hair, and drawn-on face. You may choose to improvise on this 3-D look.

YOU WILL NEED		
20 sheets of cream, heavyweight, drawing/printmaking paper, 8 x 10 inches (20.5 x 25.5 cm) and 2 sheets, 7 x 9 inches (18 x 23.5 cm)	Pencil	Hole punch
	Craft glue	Awl
	Acrylic paint	Ruler
2 pieces of matte board, 8 x 10 inches (20.5 x 25.5 cm), ⅛ inch (3 mm) thick,	Pink cord	Sea sponge
	Scrapbook paper (cream, yellow, blue, green, pink) 4-inch paper doily, gold stars	Scissors
2 pieces of white, lightweight, acid-free drawing paper, 9 x 12 inches (23.5 x 30.5 cm)		Protective sealer
	Black, acid-free, fine-point ink pen	Bone folder or spoon for burnishing

2 For the front cover, center the 8 x 9-inch square of matte board onto the white 9 x 12-inch drawing paper. One-fourth inch to one side, place the ¾-inch strip of board. Place them both on top of a strip of cloth on the paper and glue. Cut a ¼-inch strip from the large piece.

3 Fold over the corners and glue them to the board. Then fold the paper at the top and the bottom of the cover (the glue tabs or flaps) over the corner fold and onto the board and glue. Be sure to burnish these folds after gluing to ensure a smooth edge. Fold the remaining extra side of paper over what will be the outside edge of the cover and glue. Repeat with the back cover.

4 Using a sea sponge, dab acrylic paint onto the covers and inside edges where you have folded the cover paper over. Let this dry for several hours, then spray with a protective paint sealer. Let this dry for an hour.

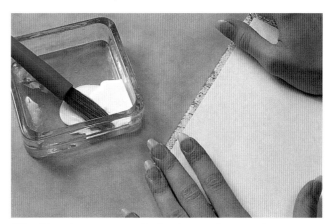

5 Glue the two 7 x 9-inch pieces of cream, heavy-weight paper onto the inside covers. Press firmly and burnish with the back of a spoon or a bone folder to get rid of all lumps and air bubbles.

6 Assemble the album by sandwiching the papers between the boards so that the holes match up. Thread the cord from the back to the front of each hole and tie it into a bow.

Heart Book Necklace

DESIGN: **JULIA MONROE**

A dazzling gift for Valentine's Day or just to say "I love you," sneak this tiny sweet surprise into an empty champagne glass or a box of chocolates.

1 Take one square of paper, wrong side up, and fold it in half diagonally. Turn paper right side up, and fold it crosswise both ways. Crease folds well. Open square back up. Pinch the corners of the diagonal and bring them together, creating a square. This folded piece is the first page of your book. Repeat with the remaining three squares of paper to form the other three pages of the book.

YOU WILL NEED
4 pieces of paper for the pages, 3¾ inches (9.5 cm) square
matte board for covers, 2 x 4-inches (5 x 10 cm)
2 x 4-inch piece of suede for cover
15 inches (38.5 cm) of silk ribbon
2 jump rings, ¼ inch (1 cm) in diameter
24-inch (62 cm) chain
Pencil
Scissors
Small paintbrush
Craft knife
Craft glue

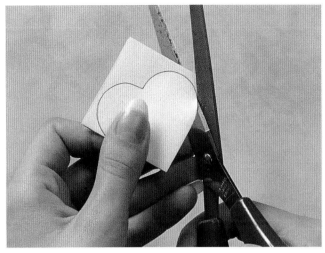

2 Draw a heart onto the folded page (it should now measures 2 inches square) lining up the point of the heart with the folded point of the page. With scissors, cut off only the top curved portion of the page. Repeat, tracing the heart and cutting the other three pages.

3 Stack and glue together the four folded pages that you made. One at a time, using craft glue, spread glue on a folded heart and press a second heart on top. Repeat until all four hearts are glued together.

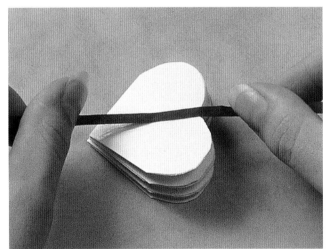

4 To attach the ribbon, spread a thin line of glue down the center of the top heart. Press the ribbon into the glue. Flip the text block over and spread a thin line of glue down the center of the bottom heart. Fold the ribbon up around the heart and press it into the glue so that the free ends of the ribbon are at the top of the heart.

5 On the the matte board trace around the heart-shaped pages and cut out two hearts. Do the same on the suede. Using the gold ink and paintbrush, paint the edge of the matte board hearts. Let dry.

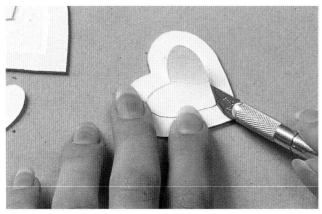

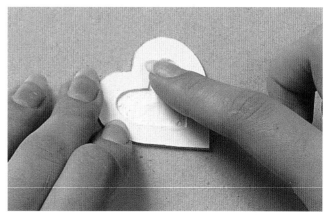

6 Draw a smaller heart on the boards. Using the craft knife, cut half-way through the matte board. Peel off the top layers of the matte board to form a recessed area.

7 Using your finger, spread a very thin layer of glue on the first matte board heart. Make sure the glue is in the recessed area and is spread all the way to the edges of the heart.

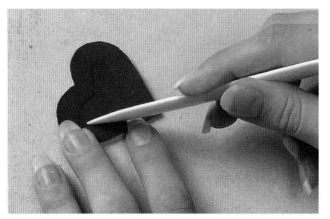

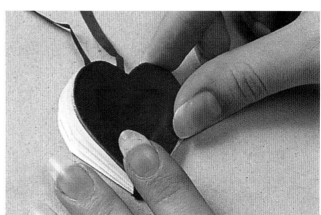

8 Lay a suede heart on top of the glue and firmly press the suede down into the recessed area. Repeat for the second cover.

9 To attach the covers, spread a thin layer of glue on the back of a cover. Press firmly to the text block. Attach the remaining cover to the other side. Attach jump rings by sliding one onto a ribbon and knotting the ribbon tightly around the jump ring. Keep the jump ring next to the heart while tying the knot. Do the same with the other jump ring on the other ribbon. Attach the chain to the jump rings. Tie the ends of the ribbon together into a bow to keep the book shut. The ribbon may be untied to open the book.

VARIATIONS

If desired, you can decorate the heart by gluing a small picture in the cover's recessed area. Or use a fine brush and the gold ink to add filigree swirls around the recessed area. A small flat charm or silk flower may also be glued into the recessed area. When choosing the decoration, just remember that too much bulk on the cover may prevent the book from opening all the way, so choose flat items as embellishment.

TIP: There is a variety of ways to add text to star books. Pages may be printed by a computer. One sheet of paper can be cut up to make the four squares for the star book. Calligraphy or rubber stamping may be added after cutting the pages. Text that continues from one page to the next is easiest to add after the pages have been glued together. The text can be written before the pages are glued but you must remember to glue them together in the right order.

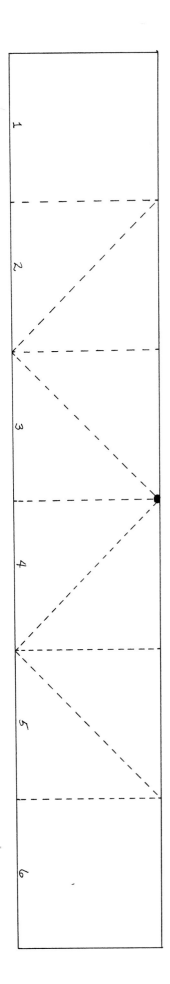

Accordion Center-Fold-Out

DESIGN: **DORIS ARNDT**

A delightful petite gift book, the accordion fold-out offers a surprise of a poem, sketches, or a random thought when unfolded.

YOU WILL NEED

2 pieces of thin cardboard or matte board, 2½ inches (6.5 cm) square

2 pieces of decorative paper, 3½ inches (9 cm) square

Craft glue

Card stock or heavy drawing paper, 2½ x 15 inches (6.5 x 38.5 cm)

15 inches (39 cm) of ribbon, ¼ inch (6 mm) wide

4 inches (10.2 cm) of ribbon, ¼ inch wide

Small piece of cellophane tape

Pencil

Ruler

Scoring tool (large paper clip or bone folder)

Scissors

1 Center and glue one of the pieces of cardboard onto the back on one of the pieces of decorative paper. Fold in the corners of the paper and glue. Fold over the top, bottom, and sides of the paper and glue into place on the cover board. Repeat these steps with the other piece of cardboard and decorative paper. Set aside.

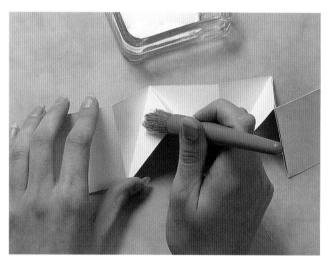

3 Glue each pair of triangles (those in the same square) together.

VARIATIONS

The text block can be turned so that the center folds up instead of out. The size of this book can be adapted. The number of panels could also be adjusted to create a longer, more paneled book. Create two text blocks and glue the first and the last panels together (wrong side to wrong side to wrong side), giving you a double fold-out. You could even flip one of the blocks upside-down and have sections that fold up as well as down.

2 Mark and score the text block along the long edge in 2½-inch intervals, making six panels, each 2½ x 2½ inches. Refer to the diagram and fold as follows:

Panel 1: Leave plain, valley fold along the vertical scored line.
Panel 2: Mountain fold from the top left corner to the bottom right corner. Valley fold on the vertical scored line.
Panel 3: Mountain fold from the bottom left corner to the upper right corner. Valley fold on the vertical scored line.
Panel 4: Repeat panel #2.
Panel 5: Repeat panel #3.
Panel 6: Leave plain.

4 Glue or tape the short length of ribbon onto the back (in the "V") of the middle text block. Tape slightly to one side of the center-top of the text block.

Doris Arndt has used stamps, sketches, and watercolors to create the designs in this book. Stickers, free-hand drawings, or just text may enhance each page to your liking. You may consider making them as "placecards" for a small but special dinner party or anniversary. The name of the couple and the occasion are revealed when the interior fold is pulled down.

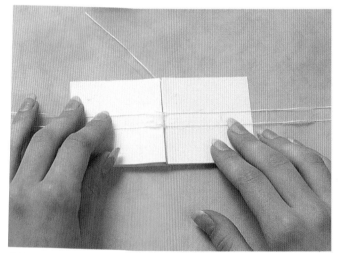

5 Fold the text block into a square. The side edges of the first and last panels should point forward. Hold the ribbon down to the inside of the front of the text block, so that it hangs out the bottom. Fold the long piece of ribbon in half. Place the fold at the back of the folded text block and glue one-half of the ribbon to ⟨...⟩ t block.

6 Glue the covers to the front and back of the ribbon-wrapped text block. Trim the ribbon ends and tie off in a bow.

Folded-Cover Feather Journal

DESIGN: **PAULA BEARDELL KRIEG**

This attractive journal is distinctive because of its removable cover. If the interior becomes filled, take out the old and replace with a fresh signature. This method of folding paper over boards is virtually identical to the brown paper bag book covers that many of us made for our elementary school textbooks.

YOU WILL NEED

16 sheets of assorted papers, 8½ x 14 inches (22 x 36 cm) Suggestions: Use graph paper, writing paper, drawing paper, decorative paper, and colored paper.

Elephant hide paper, or any sturdy heavyweight paper, 14 x 27 inches (36 x 69 cm)

2 cover boards, 8½ x 7¼ inches (22 x 18.5 cm)

Decorative elements for the front cover, such as old buttons, loose beads, feathers, paper, and single earrings

30 inches (77 cm) of waxed thread

30 inches of ribbon or cord

Scoring tool (bone folder, large paper clip)

Craft knife

Ruler

Awl

Straight sewing needle

Scissors that make deckled edges

1 Fold eight of the text papers in half, one at a time. Slip one inside another until the eight sheets are nested together, forming one signature. Repeat with the eight remaining sheets of paper, so that there are now two separate signatures. When nesting the sheets together be attentive to the arrangement of the various papers, so as to create interesting contrast between pages.

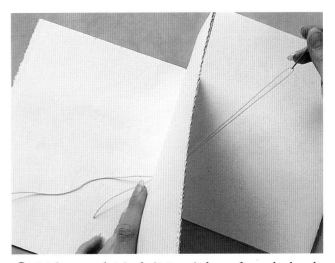

2 Make a mark 1 inch (2.5 cm) down from the head, 1 inch up from the tail, and a third mark directly in the middle of the signature crease. Poke holes through the marks with a pushpin or awl, and repeat with the second signature. Pass the threaded needle from the inside to the outside of the middle hole of the first signature, leaving a 4-inch (10 cm) tail inside the signature. Line up the spine of the second signature with the spine of the first signature, making sure that the holes match up. Pass the needle from the outside to the inside middle of the second signature. Sew up to and out of the top hole of the second signature, then sew into the outside of the top hole of the first signature, passing to the inside of the interior of the second signature. Bring the needle down to the inside bottom hole of the first signature, pass the needle from inside to the outside of this bottom hole, then press the needle into the outside of the bottom hole, going towards the interior middle of the second signature. Sew back into the middle hole of the second signature, ending in the middle hole of the interior of the first signature. Tie a knot with both ends of the thread and trim, leaving a 1-inch tail on each end.

3 Measure the thickness of the spine of the sewn signatures. It should measure out to be about ⅜ inch (1.3 cm). Fold and score the 27 inch (69 cm) length of the cover paper in half. Reopen the paper to its full length. Create a second fold ⅜ inch away from and parallel to the middle fold. Again, reopen the cover piece to its full 27-inch length. These two folds will define the spine of the book and accommodate the thickness of the two sewn signatures. Fold up a flap 3 inches (7.5 cm) from the bottom across the entire 27-inch length of the cover piece.

4 Slip the cover boards into the pockets that these flaps create, one on either side of the spine. The taller edge of the board should be parallel to the spine folds. Fold the head of the cover down snug over the cover boards, creating an even flap folded down across the entire 27-inch length of the cover. Leaving the cover boards enveloped inside the top and bottom flaps, position the cover boards so that one is directly to the left of the spine, and the other is aligned to the right of the spine. Score and fold the two outer edges of the cover over the boards.

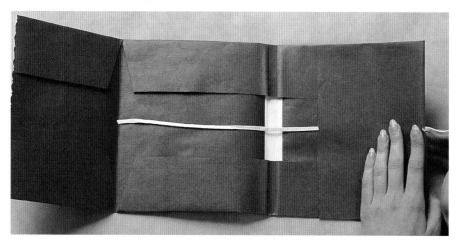

5 Remove the boards from the book cover. At the middle of the fore-edge fold of both the front and back covers, snip away a small triangle so as to accommodate the book tie. Replace cover boards inside the cover flaps on either side of the spine. Fold back down the front and back over edges.

6 Thread the book tie from the front fore-edge cut, leaving an 8-inch (20.5 cm) tail, passing the cord in front of the cover boards and back out through the hole in the folded edge of the cover. Nestle the spine of the sewn signatures into the inside spine of the cover. Slide the first leaf of the first signature into the flap of the front cover and slide the last leaf of the second signature into the flap of the back cover. Fold the book closed. Tie the tie. As desired, add decorative elements to the front cover.

Stitched Web Book with Dangles

DESIGN: **DORIS ARNDT**

This simple stitching creates an attractive web design, enhanced by baubles of your choosing. Folding the text pages double provides extra thickness and sturdiness, as well as an elegant quality to the entire book.

YOU WILL NEED

10 pieces of text-weight paper, 4¼ x 11 inches (11 x 28 cm)

2 pieces of card stock, 4¼ X 11 inches

Piece of coordinating art paper, like mulberry, approximately 4¼ x 2 inches (11 x 5 cm)

Scraps of card stock to protect the cover when clamping

Craft glue

34 inches (87 cm) of waxed linen thread

Beads with a hole large enough to hold the waxed lined thread

Jump rings

Charms, bells, etc.—anything you want to dangle from your book

Scoring tool

Small brush with water

Three small binder clips

Ruler

Pencil

Awl

Blunt large-eyed needle (tapestry needle)

Needle-nose pliers

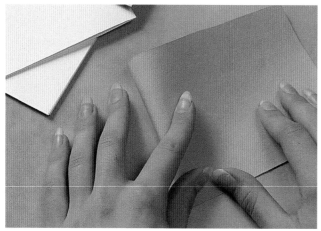

1 Fold the text pieces and the card stock pieces in half 4¼ high x 5½ inches wide (11 x 14 cm). Stack the text pieces into a neat stack inside the cover pieces with the folds of the covers at the fore edge and the folds on the text pieces at the spine. Lay aside for the moment.

2 Use a small brush dipped in water and a ruler to "draw" a waterline along the long edges of the decorative art paper.

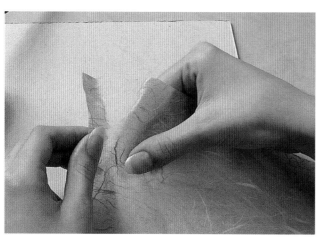

3 Let the water soak in a few moments and tear off the paper along the edges, giving it a feathered appearance. Let dry.

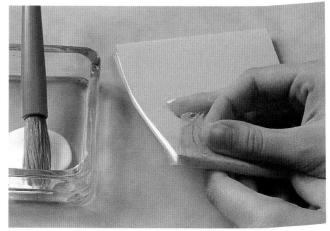

4 When dry, glue the paper to the front cover and fold the paper around the spine to the back cover. Glue this also and let dry.

5 On the back of the book stack, ⅜ inch from the spine edge, mark hole placement at 1½ inches (4 cm) and 2¾ (7 cm) from the bottom edge. Mark another hole at ¾ inches (2 cm) from the spine and 2⅛ inches (6 cm) from the bottom edge. Clamp the book stack on the top, bottom, and fore edge with the binder clips. Keep the book stack clamped until the book is stitched.

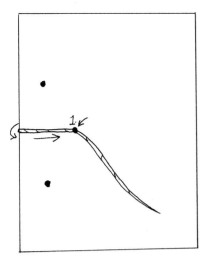 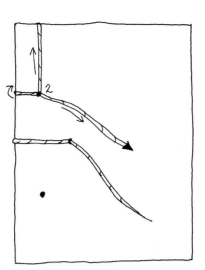 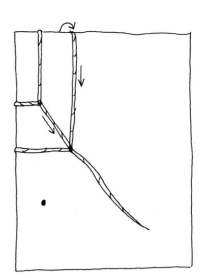

6 Using the waxed thread and needle, start on the front of the book and go through hole 1 to the back of the book and leave a "tail" of waxed linen of about 5 inches (13 cm). On the back, come around the spine to the front and through hole 1 to the back of the book.

7 On the back of the book , go through hole 2 to the front of the book, around the spine to the back of the book and through the same hole. On the front of the book go around the top edge of the book to the back and through the same hole to the front.

8 On the front, go through hole 1 to the back. On the back, go around the top of the book to the front and through hole 1 to the back.

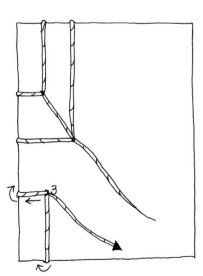 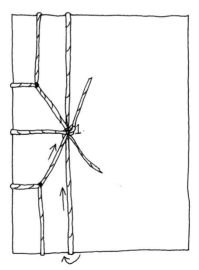

9 On the back, go through hole 3 to the front and around the spine to the back. On the front, go around the bottom edge to the back and through the same hole to the front. On the front, go through hole 1 to the back.

10 On the back, go around the bottom edge to the front. Stitch the waxed linen underneath the center stitch (rather than going through the hole) to anchor the waxed linen and tie the waxed linen off in a square knot using both ends of the waxed linen.

TIP: Score the cover 1 inch away from the spine to ease the opening of the book.

VARIATION

Attach some charms to two jump rings by twisting the jump ring apart and sliding the hoops onto the jump ring and twisting the ring back together. Slide a few beads onto one of the "tails". Attach one of the jump rings with charms using the following loop. Repeat with the other tail.

Matchbook Cover Book

DESIGN: **DORIS ARNDT**

This clever book hearkens back to another era,
when thoughts, poetry, and letters were carried
close to the heart and closed to prying eyes.

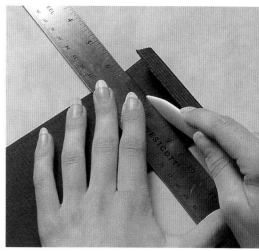

1 On the back of the corrugated card stock (the smooth side) mark and score a line ¾ inch (2 cm) away from the left side along the narrow edge.

4 Using the needle and thread, stitch the cover to the text stack. Bring the needle up through the bottom hole in back and pull around the edge, coming back through the same hole, then stitch up through the top hole. Bring the needle from back around the side back into the top hole. Tie off in a square knot on the back when you have completed the stitching. Remove the clamps.

YOU WILL NEED

Corrugated card stock (fluted front and smooth back—available at most art supply stores), 3 x 10 inches (7.5 x 25.5 cm) with the flutes running vertically

18 pieces of text-weight paper, 3 x 4 inches (7.5 x 10 cm)

12 inches (30.5 cm) of waxed thread

Tassel on cord

Craft glue

Sealing wax

Binder clips

Scoring tool

Awl

Needle

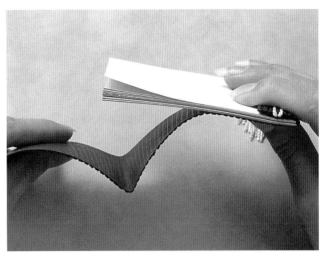

2 Mark two holes ½ inch (1.5 cm) away from the left edge at 1 inch (2.5 cm) and 2 inches (5 cm) from the bottom (holes are 1 inch apart). Pierce the signature at the marks to create holes.

3 Stack the text pieces in a straight pile and lay the cover piece on top with the right side (fluted side) facing the stack and the scored line to the left. Secure with two clips, one at the top edge, and one at the bottom edge.

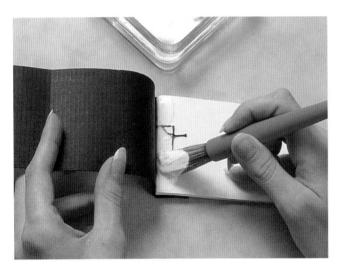

5 Fold the cover piece along the scored line back over onto itself (this makes the area that the cover will tuck into) to the left and around the spine of your book. Open the cover piece back up. In the fold-back area (before the spine area), if you choose to decorate with tassel, loop the cord around the cover and place the tassel through the loop. Pull up securely with the tassel hanging out the bottom. Apply glue to the back of the cover over the stitching to hold it all securely into place.

6 Continue folding the cover over the spine and around the text stack to the front of the book and tuck underneath the flap at the left (you may need to trim off some excess from the cover). Apply the sealing wax to the front, pressing it into the tassel cords to add a decorative touch.

TIP: Sealing wax comes in stick, tablet, and pebble form. It must be heated to be applied. Allow to cool.

Ornament Books

DESIGN: **DORIS ARNDT**

*These variations of an origami or star book
can bejewel a window, a holiday tree, or anywhere
they can hang freely, lending a festive air
to their surroundings. Open them completely,
as if turning inside out, and they become snowflakes.*

1 Fold a text piece in half and open. Fold
the same text piece in half in the other
direction and open. Fold the same text
piece in half along one diagonal. Pinch the
corners of the diagonal and bring them
together in the center, making a smaller
square. Repeat these steps with the other
text pieces.

YOU WILL NEED

3 pieces of text-weight paper,
4 inches (10.2 cm) square

2 pieces of card stock, 2 inches (5 cm) square

25 inches (63.5 cm) of ribbon,
⅛ inch (3 mm) wide

Craft glue

One bead with a hole large enough to hold the
doubled ribbon snugly

Scoring tool

Pencil

Craft knife

VARIATION

This project is actually modeled
after origami books. To make a more
traditional origami book, don't cut the
text stack and card stock, but leave them
intact. Finish the book as above.

2 Glue the squares on top of each other, making sure to line up all the pages so that the connected parts of the papers are on the bottom, the open ends at the top.

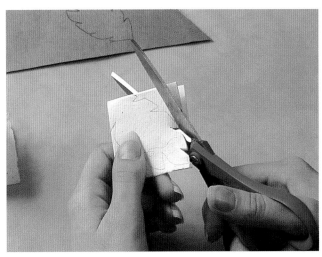

3 Draw a shape onto the front side of one of the card stock pieces. Trace the same shape onto the other card stock piece, and the inside text pages. Make sure the shape is facing the proper direction on all the pages and cut out the desired shape through all layers.

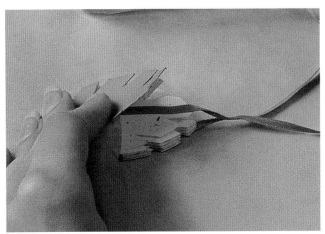

4 Glue the ribbon around the glued stack of pages on both sides of the stack, leaving tails of equal length on both ends. Glue one card stock piece to each side of the page stack. Make sure they line up.

5 Slide the bead onto both ends of the ribbon. Cutting the ribbon ends to a sharp angle can make sliding the bead on easier.

6 Tie off at the ends with an overhand knot. Slide the bead along the ribbon to the knot, open the book so that the covers touch and slide the bead back down to the book to hold the book open for the full snowflake or star-like effect.

TIP: Use decorative scissors to trim along the outer edges after folding and gluing the text stack, but before gluing the covers and ribbon.

How to Fly in Dreams, Gwen Diehn

Magic, Joyce Brodsky

BIRDS
PARAKEET
PARROT
FINCH
GOLDEN FINCH
ZEBRA FINCH
QUAIL
DOVE
CHICKEN
TURKEY
CANARY
GOOSE
DUCK

Les oiseaux
la perruche
le perroquet
le finche
le finche d'or
le finche zebrent
la caille
la colombe
le poulet
le dindon
le canari
l'oie
le canard

French for Shoppers, Gwen Diehn

B R E

Pencil Spine, *Beth Weiss*

Shuttle, *Gwen Diehn*

a friendship begins.

Checkerd Pocket Accordion-Fold, *Beth Weiss*

Circle of Friendship, *Joyce Brodsky*

THE!

Breath In, Breath Out, *Gwen Diehn*

Wire-Bound Book with Curlicues

A brilliant and unique way to bind a book—the copper wire looks like jewelry and adds the perfect balance of dazzle to a simple tome.

DESIGN: **DORIS ARNDT**

YOU WILL NEED

10 pieces of text paper, 5½ x 8½ inches (14 x 22 cm)	3 small binder clips (available at office supply stores)
2 pieces of cover stock, 5½ x 8½ inches	Ruler
36 inches (92.5 cm) of 20-gauge copper wire	Pencil
3 small pieces of scrap card stock	Awl
Scoring tool	Long-nose pliers with a cutting edge

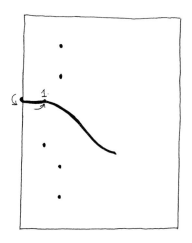

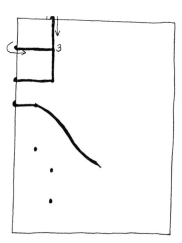

1 Fold all text pieces in half to 5½ inches high x 4½ inches wide (14 x 11 cm). Fold the cover stock in half, to 5½ inches high x 4½ inches wide. Stack the pages in between the two cover pieces, with the loose edges of both the text pages and the card stock at the spine and the folded edges at the fore edge. This will give you doubled pages that have an elegant feel and turn easily.

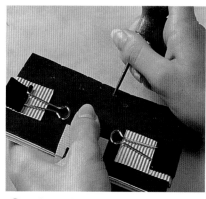

2 Clamp book stack with binder clips at top, bottom and fore edges. Make sure text pages and covers align. Use scrap card stock between the clips and the book covers. Keep the stack clamped until the wiring is finished. On the back of the book stack, mark holes ½ inch (1.5 cm) from the spine edge at 2½ inches (6.5 cm) and 3 inches (7.5 cm). Mark another set of holes at 1 inch (2.5 cm) in from the spine at 1, 2, 3, and 4½ inches. Pierce holes at the marks with an awl.

3 With the wire, stitch the book. As you are working keep the wire tight and flat so as to give a nice appearance.

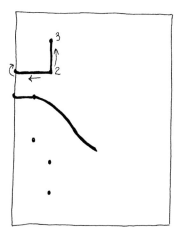

4 On the back of the book go through hole 2 to the front of the book. Go around the spine to the back and through the same hole to the front of the book. Go to hole 3 and through to the back of the book. Come around the spine to the front of the book and back through the same hole to the back of the book.

5 Go around the top edge of the book to the front and through the same hole to the back of the book.

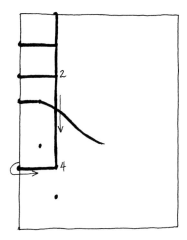

6 On the back of the book go through hole 2 and through to the front and through hole 4 to the back of the book. From the back of the book go around the spine to the front and through the same hole to the back again.

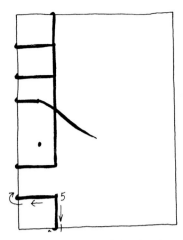

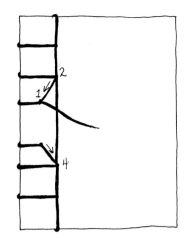

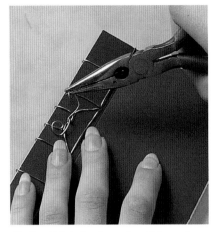

7 On the back of the book go through hole 5 and around the spine to the back of the book and through the same hole to the front. Go around the bottom of the book to the back and through the same hole to the front of the book.

9 Go through hole 4 to the back of the book. You may need to enlarge the hole a bit to accommodate the wire. On the back of the book go through hole 2 to the front of the book. You may need to enlarge this hole a bit also. Go through hole 1 to the back of the book.

11 With both ends of the wire on the front of the book, twist both wires together securely, close to the book. Trim the ends of the wire evenly at about 2 inches with the wire cutters. Grasp one wire end with the pliers and twist toward the spine creating a curlicue. Flatten so that it lies parallel to the book cover. Repeat with the other wire end.

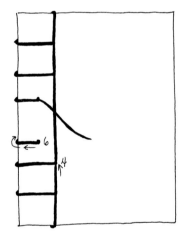

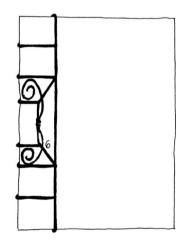

8 On the front of the book go through hole 4 to the back of the book. On the back go through hole 6 to the front of the book. Go around the spine to the back of the book and out the same hole to the front.

10 On the back of the book go through hole 6 to the front of the book.

12 Score the front cover 1¼ inches (3.5 cm) away from the spine to ease the opening of the book.

Coptic-Bound Sketch Journal

The Coptic binding method used for this book is the earliest known binding of the codex format, dating back to fourth-century Egypt. It is sturdy and will allow you to open the book flat.

DESIGN: **GWEN DIEHN**

YOU WILL NEED

Medium-weight paper for pages 4 x 11 inches (10 x 28 cm); each sheet will be folded in half, yielding 4 x 5½ inches (10 x 14 cm)

2 sheets of chip board or cover board ¼ inch (1 cm) taller and ½ inch (1.5 cm) wider than the pages

2 pieces of decorative paper, the size of the cover board plus 1 inch (2.5 cm)

Craft glue

2 sheets of decorative paper, as end paper 3¾ x 5 inches (9.5 x 13 cm)

2 yards (1.85 m) of waxed cotton thread

Pencil

Scissors

Ruler

Glue brush

Scoring tool (bone folder, paper clips)

Awl

Curved needle

1 Fold text pages in half so that each one measures 4 x 5½ inches. Slip the pages inside each other in groups of eight, which will give you five signatures.

2 Place the cover boards on top of the decorative paper. Draw around each board to make glue tabs, or you may lightly make an indention with the bone folder. Cut the corner tips of the paper off, leaving a bit of paper as thick as the cover board.

3 Spread glue on the paper with a glue brush and place the board within the marks you have made, pressing down. Then take one of the glue tabs and fold over onto the board, pressing with your bone folder. Bring the adjacent glue tab over the board and smooth and press the paper with the scoring tool.

4 Spread glue all over the undecorated side of each end paper, center, and press down over the cover flaps.

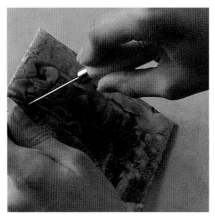

5 Hold the two covers the way they will be when the book is finished. Mark where you want the holes, at least ½ inch (1.5 cm) in from the edge. At the marks of each cover, twist the awl in a screw-like motion and press straight down.

6 Gather the signatures together and place them next to one of the covers as they will be when the book is finished. Holding the book tightly, use a pencil to draw a line down from signature fold to signature fold below each of the cover holes. The marks will indicate where to poke the holes in the signatures. Open the signatures and punch holes at the marks.

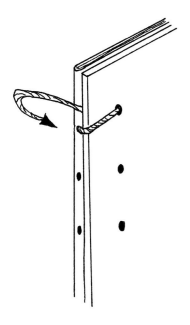

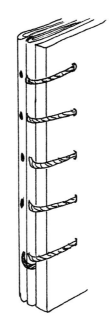

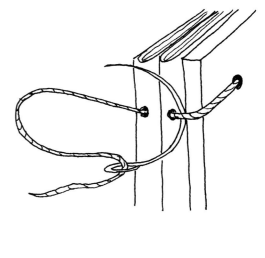

7 Pick up either cover and the first signature next to that cover. Put needle into first hole from either end of signature from the inside. Pull thread through. Reach with needle around cover and put needle into first hole of cover from outside. Pull thread through between cover and first signature. Always pull parallel to the spine or edge of book.

8 Pull needle back into the first hole of the signature from outside. Continue until all the cover holes are sewn and cover is joined at first signature. Stop when you come to the last cover hole. Do not go into the first cover hole of the first signature. Instead, pick up the second signature and go into the first hole from the outside. From the inside of the first signature, put needle into the second hole and pull thread to the outside.

9 From the outside, use the curve of the needle to scoop the little pieces of thread that is between the cover and the first signature. Pull the needle back into the second hole of the second signature from the outside. The little scoop stitch is what holds the second signature to the first signature.

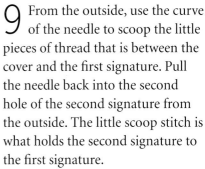

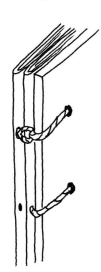

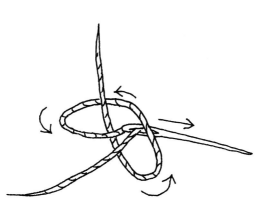

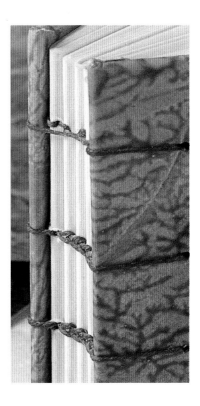

10 Always be sure to scoop the thread that is between the signature you are sewing and the one you just finished sewing. Sew the rest of the signatures.

11 Sew the back cover to the last signature in the same way you sewed the first cover to the first signature. When you finish the last hole, tie off the thread on the inside of signature.

Fruit Recipe Book

DESIGN: **JULIA MONROE**

This project goes to show that a "book" may take on many shapes and forms. Make an entire fruit basket full and give as a gift that will be proudly displayed.

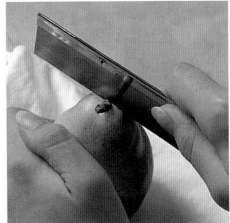

1 Using the craft saw, carefully cut the fruit in half. Hold the fruit firmly in or on a folded towel for a better grip. Draw the blade slowly through the fruit toward you. Turn the fruit as you cut if the fruit is wider than the saw blade. Cut on one side of the wire stem. The stem may be removed by twisting and pulling firmly if it interferes with the saw cut. You may reattach the stem to one side of the fruit if you want by sticking it into the top of one of the fruit halves.

VARIATION

Instead of using two clasps, a hinge may be used with one clasp. The resulting book will not extend but can be read as a normal book by turning pages. If desired, you can also paint the outside of the fruit with non-tradtional designs such as checks, stripes, or flowers.

YOU WILL NEED

Polystyrene fruit, 2 to 3 inches (5 to 7.5 cm) tall	Artificial fruit leaves	Scissors
Scrap paper	Craft saw	Ruler
80-lb. watercolor paper for the text	Folded towel	Craft Knife
Gold cord	Pencil	Glue
2 brass clasps, 1/2 inch (1.3 cm)	Acrylic paints	Tape
Small brass nails	Paint brush	Pliers

2 Cut out a strip of paper for the text (see tip). Fold the strip fan-style to make the eight pages of the accordion fold strip. Turn the strip right side up. The right side is the side that has four valley folds. Lay one piece of the cut fruit on the folded strip and trace around it. Paint the cut side of the fruit with acrylic paints. Cut out the pattern you made about ³⁄₁₆ inch (2 mm) inside the line you drew to make the pattern a little smaller than the actual fruit. Open the text strip. Turn the strip right side up with the first fold to your left being a "valley" fold. Write your recipe on the text paper. Embellish with drawings or rubber-stamped images if you wish.

3 Glue the back of the first page of the accordion strip to the inside front of the fruit: spread craft glue on the inside of the cut fruit; press the folded accordion strip firmly to the glue. Repeat to glue the text strip to the other cut fruit.

5 Tape the fruit together temporarily with tape to assist in attaching the hardware. Check placement of the clasp to the widest part of the fruit. Use pliers to carefully bend the clasp to fit the curve of the fruit better. Attach a clasp to the fruit by placing it on the fruit and firmly pushing in the brass nails. Attach the second clasp to the other side of the fruit. Remove the temporary tape. Glue or pin the silk leaf to the top of the fruit.

TIP: To find the right size of the text paper strip, measure across the widest part of the pattern. Multiply this number by eight and then subtract 1½ inches (4 cm). This is the length of your text strip. Measure the height of the pattern you made and add ½ inch (1.5 cm). This is the height of the text strip.

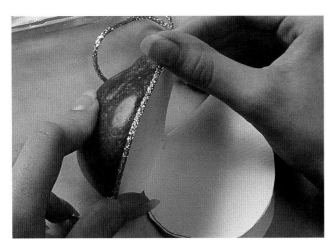

4 With craft glue, glue a piece of gold cord around the text strip on each half of fruit. Let dry thoroughly before closing the fruit book.

Stab-Bound Star Book

DESIGN: **NICOLE TUGGLE**

An elegantly-bound album, this book is a lovely piece to leave out on a coffee table.
You can match the cover paper in color and texture to complement your decor.

MATERIALS

2 cover boards of equal size, 6 x 9 inches (15 x 23 cm)

Decorative paper (for covers—should be relatively strong)

Text-weight paper (cut slightly smaller than the cover boards)

Thin ribbon, waxed linen, or waxed string

Craft glue

Awl

TIP: You might have to punch holes in each cover separately, depending on the thickness of the cover boards. Mark and pierce the front cover first. Stack the cover boards and mark through each hole of the front cover onto the inside of the back cover to align holes. Then pierce back cover.

1 Cut a ¾-inch (2 cm) strip from the left side of the front cover, then cut ⅛-inch (5 mm) strip from the large piece of the front cover. Place the narrow strip, now detached, to the left of the rest of the cover board, on the decorative cover paper, making sure the front cover will be even in size to the back cover. Measure, mark, and cut the paper.

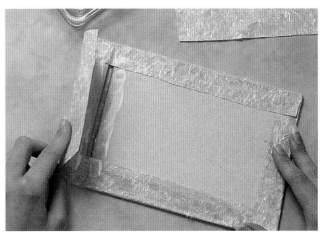

2 Cut the paper corners in a diagonal to the board corners. Glue down the shorter flap first, then bring the long flap over the board and part of the glued-down shorter flap. Eliminate bubbles or folds with your scoring tool, moving and pressing it firmly over the glued-down areas. Keep the space in the front cover, but line it up to the back cover to make sure they're still the same size. Repeat with the back, without the space.

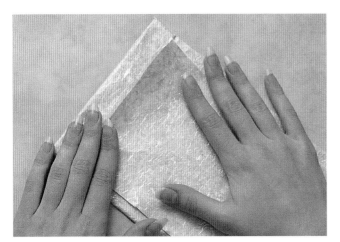

3 Glue the end papers on the inside of each cover. They can be the same color as the cover or one that will accent it nicely.

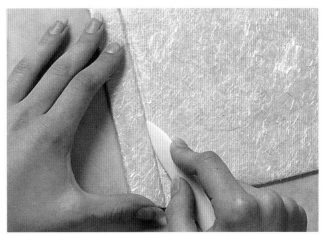

4 Flip the cover over and score the space in between the narrow strip of board and the wider part of the cover. This will ensure that the book will open easily.

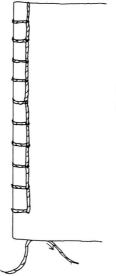

8 Start a running stitch down the book, this time stopping at each hole to wrap the thread around the left side of the book.

5 Measure out the holes on the left side of the front cover. This is really a matter of preference. An even or odd number is fine. For this book, there are 11 holes spaced ½ inch (1.5 cm) apart. Measure and mark with a pencil. Make sure the spacing between each hole is equal. Do the same with the clamped stacks of text paper. Place a sponge behind the cover and stacks to absorb the sharp tip of the awl as it goes through. Poke through each mark.

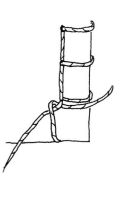

9 Continue to the bottom; wrap the thread around the bottom edge and side. The thread should be coming out of the last two holes of the back cover. Tie this with the tail left from the beginning. Cut off extra thread and poke the knot through one of the holes with the awl.

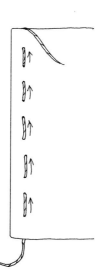

6 Your thread should be at least three times the length of the book. Hold the book together very firmly. (All holes must line up). Sew through the bottom hole, coming out the front. Leave 3 inches of thread at the back (we will use this later). Go up the book with a running stitch (down through one hole and up through the next.

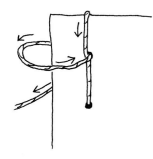

7 When you reach the top of the book, wrap the thread around the top edge and back through the first hole, then around the side and through same hole.

10 To decorate, glue a decorative bauble (here, a star) to a sheet of stiff decorative paper. You can choose the size. Place this in the center of the book and glue. Glue a frame on top of it, which you can buy or simply make by wrapping and gluing thin paper around a frame you have cut from cover board. Center this on top of the slightly smaller decorative paper square and glue.

Sands of Time Accordion Book

DESIGN: **JULIA MONROE**

This lovely art book ads a decorative touch to the shelves of a home library or study.
Record birthdays or other monumental dates on its pages.

YOU WILL NEED

Strip of 80-lb. paper, 8 x 25½ inches (20.5 x 65.5 cm) for the text strip

5 pieces of matte board, 4⅜ x 8⅛ inches (11.3 x 21.3 cm)

2 pieces of clear acetate, 4 x 7½ inches (10 x 19 cm)

1 teaspoon of fine sand

2 pieces of thin decorative cover paper, 5¾ x 9¾ inches (14.5 x 25 cm)

Pencil

Hourglass pattern (see page 76)

Craft knife

Clamps

Craft glue

Scoring tool

Clock stamp and ink pad

1 Trace the hourglass shape on three of the cover boards. Cut out with a craft knife.

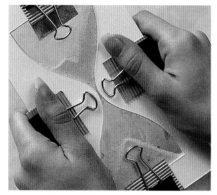

2 Try out your sand in the hourglass before gluing the cover together. Lay one hourglass piece on your work surface with a piece of acetate on top. Add a second hourglass piece. Carefully spoon ½ teaspoon of sand in the center of each half of the hourglass. Top with the remaining acetate and board. Clamp the layers tightly together and turn the hourglass to see if the sand falls freely. If necessary, the neck of the hourglass may be cut a little wider to allow the sand to pass. Take the matte board and acetate pieces apart and brush off all loose sand. Spread a thin layer of glue on one board. Press a piece of acetate to the board, then glue the second board to the acetate; repeat filling with sand. Clamp and let dry.

3 Prepare the top cover board. To make a nice covered edge around the hourglass, spread glue on one board and press it in the center of one of the pieces of thin decorative paper. Cut out the inside of the hourglass ¼ inch (1 cm) from the edge. Slit the four corners and the neck section of the hourglass. Spread craft glue on the cut edges of the paper and fold them to the inside of the hourglass. Smooth and press well.

4 Spread glue on inside of prepared board and press over the acetate. Press the cover for two hours and let glue dry thoroughly before tipping hourglass. After glue has dried, trim corners of cover paper ½ inch (1.5 cm), then glue the corners of the paper to back of board. Apply glue to the four flaps of cover paper and press smoothly over edges and back of board. For the back, glue the remaining two boards together and cover .

5 Score and fold the strip of text paper every 4¼ inches (11 cm) to make 6 equal sections. Trace the hourglass shape on the first page and cut out with a craft knife. Stamp the pages with a clock stamp or decorative stamp of your choosing.

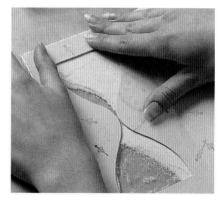

6 Matching up the hourglass cutout, glue the text strip to the inside of the front cover board. Glue the back page of the accordion strip to the back cover. Press the book overnight.

TIP: If you cannot find a sheet of acetate, clear transparency film for laser printers or even the acetate cut from an inexpensive report cover will work fine. 10-mm acetate works well and resists scratching by coarser sand. When handling acetate, avoid getting fingerprints on it. If you do, remove them with a soft tissue before assembling your book.

Japanese-Bound Picture Frame Album

DESIGN: **NICOLE TUGGLE**

This elegant album, an artful combination of textured paper and simple stitching, features a built-in frame that can house a photograph or sketch, denoting what's inside.

1 large sheet of double-sided
decorative paper

Medium-weight text paper, 8½ x 11 inches (22 x 28 cm)

2 colored text pages, 8½ x 11 inches

Waxed cotton thread

2 cover boards, 8½ x 11 inches

Awl

Needle

Hand-held hole punch

Scissors

Scoring tool

Pencil

TIP: If using a photo as cover decoration, you may want the option of substituting other photos. Instead of gluing the top of the frame to the cover, leave this unglued, so you have a space through which to slide a different photo into the frame.

2 Leaving the ¼-inch space, which will become the hinge, glue the paper onto the board. Glue the tabs, folding them over the sides of the board. From the same decorative paper or other complementing paper, cut the end paper slightly smaller than the cover and glue down over the tabs and inside of the cover.

1 Measure 1 inch (2.5 cm) in from the left side along one of the cover boards and mark with a pencil; cut along the line with a craft knife. Measure in ¼ inch (1 cm) from the left side of the large piece that remains and cut, discarding the ¼-inch strip. Place both pieces of cover board on a sheet of the decorative paper. Measure 1 inch (2.5 cm) all around for glue tabs.

3 Using the bone folder, score the hinge to define the edges. Cut a strip of decorative paper just over 2 inches wide (5 cm). You may use the other side of the double-sided paper for contrast with the cover. Glue one inch of it to the left side of the front cover, so that it reaches just to the hinged area. Wrap the rest around to the other side of the front cover and glue down. Tuck the remaining paper down and fold over to the other side.

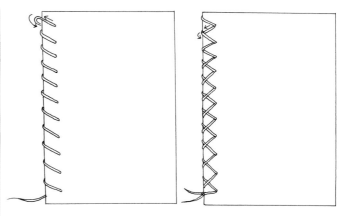

4 Measure ½ inch (1.5 cm) from the top and bottom of the left-hand side of the cover. Mark with a dot. Measure 1 inch (2.5 cm) from the dot and mark again. Continue down the length of the book until there are 11 holes. Poke each dot with an awl in a screwing motion.

6 Clamp text pages and covers together, making sure the holes line up. Starting at the back, sew through the bottom hole, coming through the front cover. Leave several inches of thread at the end. Sew around the spine of the book in an upward fashion and through the second hole in back. The thread will be coming out of the front. Continue the running stitch until thread comes out of top hole. Go around the spine and down fashion through the second to the top hole in back. Thread will be coming out the front. Continue the running stitch downward. Tie the remaining thread in a knot and trim excess. Conceal the knot by poking it through one of the holes with an awl.

5 Make same marks and measurements on your text pages. Taking a few pages at a time, punch holes with a hole punch. This will allow for thicker thread to easily go through. Collect all pages, adding one colored text page at the front and one at the back.

7 For the frame, you may use a purchased light-weight frame, or make your own, by wrapping a frame cut from matte board with decorative paper. Glue the paper as you wrap. Size the frame to the photograph or page you will be framing. Brush glue onto the back of the frame and position in the center of album. Press.

Thank You, Ellen Daugherty

Hours for the Beach, Gwen Diehn

The Effects of Plant Toxonomy, Gwen Diehn

Holiday in Green, Joyce Brodsky

Five Walks, Gwen Diehn

Sand, Kristin Cozzolino

April 3 – Day 1 – Work day
cleared brush-rose
bushes and unidentified
stuff —

April 4 – Day 2
Have a few odd bites,
very itchy. Seems
early for insects —

poison ivy!
that's impossible, I
never get poison ivy!

Cures, Gwen Diehn with Ann Turkle

Bottom all along here

Wedding Album

DESIGN: **GWEN DIEHN**

A beautiful memory album with delicate petal paper, silk ribbon, and sturdy text pages inside, this book can be used as a scrapbook as well as a more formal album. The heavyweight paper supports photos, letters, or pasted-in clippings.

80-lb. cover stock or heavier than copier stock, 9¼ x 11 inches (23.5 x 28 cm)

2 pieces of cover board the size of the text pages plus ¼ inch (1 cm) in length and minus ¾ inch (2 cm) in width. (For an 8½ x 11-inch page size the cover boards must be 9 x 11¼ inches)

1 piece of thin cloth, 2 inches (5 cm) wide and 4 inches (10 cm) longer than the length of the cover boards, to use as a hinge for the front cover

2 pieces of decorative paper to cover the cover boards, 2 inches bigger than the cover boards all around

2 pieces of decorative paper for end papers, ½ inch (1.3 cm) shorter than both the length and width of the cover boards

Craft glue

A length of thin ribbon 5 times the length of the spine of the book (cover board length)

Scoring tool

Craft knife

Steel straightedge

Awl, hole punch or hand drill with ⅛-inch bit

Glue brush

Pencil

4 large clips

Board to put under the book while drilling holes

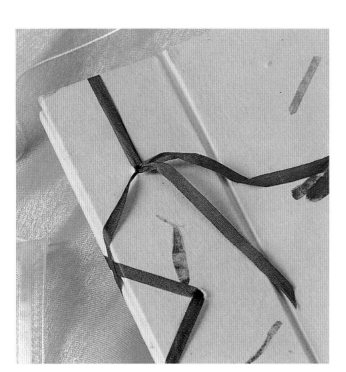

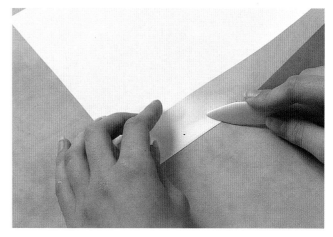

1 Score a line 1¼ inches (3.5 cm) in from the left edge on each text page. Then fold the section to the left of the score under the main part of the page. Use the bone folder to burnish all folds until they are crisp. Stack up the text pages to form a text block, with all the folded edges to the left.

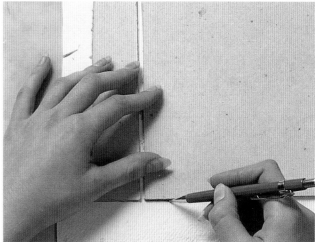

2 Use a craft knife and straightedge to cut a strip 1¼ inches wide from the left edge of the front cover board. This piece will be hinged to the bigger piece of the front cover. In order for the cover to hinge easily, cut a second strip the thickness of the cover boards plus ¹⁄₁₆ inch from the big piece of the front cover. Place the two pieces of the cover on the inside of the front cover paper. Leave a gap the thickness of the cover board plus ¹⁄₁₆ inch between the spine edge strip and the big piece of cover board. Draw a line with the pencil and straightedge along the bottom of the cover pieces and mark the sides of the two pieces along this line. This step will help you line up the pieces after you have applied glue to the cover paper.

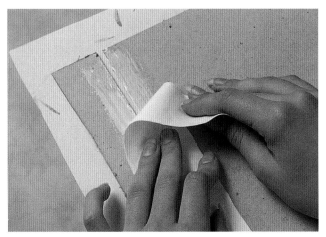

3 Brush glue onto one side of the hinge cloth and press the cloth onto the left cover piece and the big cover piece, spanning and maintaining the gap between them. You can leave the pieces of board in place on the cover paper in order to help maintain the proper gap.

4 Remove the front cover pieces with their hinge and apply glue to the entire inside of the front cover paper. Then replace the two hinged pieces along the pencil line, turning the hinged piece over so that the cloth is down. Be sure to line up the hinged piece according to the marks you made earlier on the cover paper. Press down on the hinged cover to adhere it to the paper, and then quickly fold down a triangle at each corner of the paper and burnish these corner covers thoroughly. Turn over and burnish cover paper over cover boards, using scrap paper to protect the paper from the burnishing tool. Turn back over and glue down the flaps and burnish them.

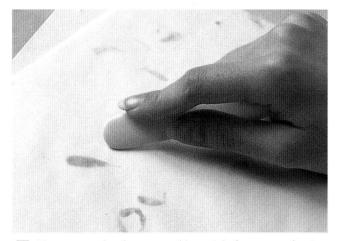

5 Turn cover back over and burnish front one final time. Cover the back cover the same way as front; do not hinge back cover. Cover entire board with the other piece of cover paper. The two covers will be the same size. A piece of front cover board equal in size to the gap between the two pieces of front cover board has been cut away. Apply glue to one side of the end papers, and press them to the insides of the covers, burnishing thoroughly. Wrap boards in waxed paper and press under a pile of books in order to help them dry flat.

6 When the covers are dry, line up covers and text block just as they will be in the finished album. Clip book together so that nothing can move (put pieces of scrap paper between cover and clip to protect cover paper), and use the pencil to mark holes along smaller (spine edge) section of front cover. The holes should be ½ inch from the spine edge and an inch from each other and from the top and bottom edges of book. Drill marked holes through both covers and text block at one time, making sure the clips hold firmly and everything stays perfectly lined up.

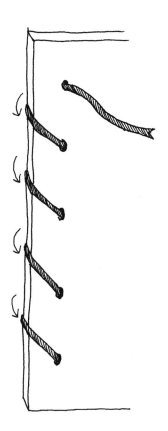

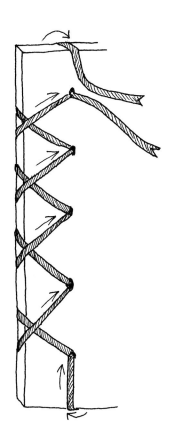

7 To stitch the book, keep everything clamped. Push the ribbon through the first hole at the top of the book (use a blunt needle to help push the ribbon through the hole if necessary) and simply loop it through each hole, spiraling to the bottom of the book.

8 After going through the bottom hole, bring the ribbon around the bottom edge of the book and go back into the bottom hole. Now spiral up the book, going into the same hole. The ribbon will cross at or near the spine edge of the book. When you reach the top of the book again, take the ribbon over the top and bring it toward the original end of ribbon that is hanging there.

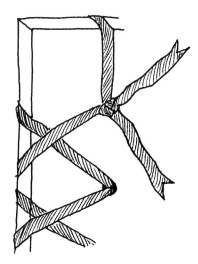

9 Tie the two ends of ribbon together and trim them.

Shell Book

DESIGN: **JULIA MONROE**

Delicate and lovely, this ode to the sea harbors a surprise inside.

YOU WILL NEED

30 pieces of paper, 9½ x 8½ inches (24.5 x 28 cm) for the text

2 pieces of matte board, 9½ x 8½ inches

2 pieces of decorative paper, 9½ x 8½ inches, such as unryu, for the cover

4 pieces of thin cotton or silk fabric, 1 x 4 inches (2.5 x 10 cm), cut on the bias

2 pieces thin card stock, 9½ x 8½ inches for the end papers and cover lining

36 inches (92.5 cm) of strong waxed thread

Sea shells, no more than ½ inch thick so the book cover can be opened easily

½-inch-diameter faux pearl

Shell pattern

Pencil

Scissors

Paper clips

Ruler

Craft knife

Craft glue

Blunt needle, such as a tapestry needle

Drill with ⁵⁄₆₄-inch bit (optional)

200 grit sandpaper (optional)

Swivel-blade craft knife or hole punch to cut the page holes

1 Cut 30 sheets of paper following the shell pattern. Up to three sheets of paper can be paper-clipped together and cut out at the same time. Cut two shell-shaped pages from the decorative paper for the end papers. Place one on the top and bottom of the stack of shell pages. Using the same shell pattern, cut two shells from the matte board. With a straightedge and craft knife, cut and remove a ¼-inch (1 cm) strip from the narrowest part of one shell board as shown on the pattern.

3 Thinly spread glue on the shell board and press it to the cover paper. Spread glue on the base of the shell and press it to the paper lined up against the ¼-inch strip. Remove the strip, creating a gap that will allow the cover to fold back when the book is sewn. Glue a strip of fabric over the gap in the boards to reinforce the cover's hinges. Make sure the strip is pressed down well into the groove between the boards. Cut the cover paper ⅜ inch from the board. Clip all inside corners. Brush glue on the paper edge and firmly smooth it up and around the board edges. Creases in the paper around the corners are minimized by using thin cover paper. Repeat these steps to make the back cover board, but do not make a hinge or cut a strip.

2 Center the shell board, the ¼ inch strip and the shell base on the cover paper. Draw a pencil line around each piece so you know where to place the pieces when gluing.

4 For the cover lining, cut two shells of card stock. When cutting out the card stock, cut the shells about ¹⁄₁₆ inch smaller than the pattern. Glue this, centered, onto the inside cover, matching the fabric hinges. On the front of the book, press the fabric hinge area down against the lining hinge. Cover the inside card stock with a piece of cover paper cut to shape.

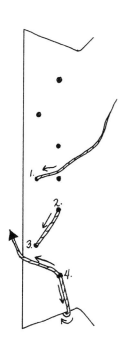

5 Place the stack of prepared text pages between the book covers. Clamp firmly together with clothespins or clamps. Using a hand drill or awl, make holes along the shell base following the placement on the pattern. Starting with hole 1, take the needle down through hole 1 and up through hole 2, leaving a 10-inch tail of thread coming out of hole 1 to tie off later. Continue stitching down through hole 3 and up through hole 4. Take the needle around the side of the book and up through the same hole again (4).

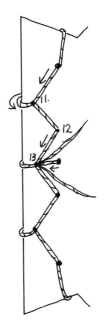

8 Take the needle around the side of the book and back up through the same hole again (10); down through hole 11. Bring the needle up around the edge of the book and back down through the same hole again (11); up through hole 12; down through hole 13; up through hole 14. Tie off the two ends of the thread in a tight knot. Add decorative shells and knot again.

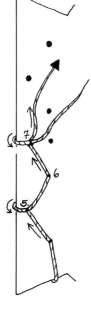

6 Stitch down through hole 5. Bring the needle up around the edge of the book and down through the same hole again (5); up through hole 6; down through hole 7.

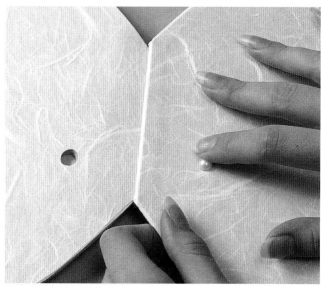

9 Draw a circle ⅛ inch larger than the pearl on the top end paper. Place a scrap of matte board between the back end paper and the back cover. This will keep you from cutting through the back cover when making the page holes for the pearl. If using a swivel blade craft knife to make the holes, cut on the circle you drew through several of the text pages. Remove the cut-out circles and work your way through the book till all pages have been cut, all the way to the back cover. Place the pearl in the hole of the pages and see if the book can be shut. If not, use the sandpaper to sand off a portion of the pearl until it fits in the hole. Then glue the pearl to the back cover in the center of the page's holes. Press the book overnight.

7 Bring the needle up around the edge of the book and down through the same hole again (7); up through hole 8; down through hole 9; up through hole 10.

Hexagonal Bee Book

DESIGN: **JULIA MONROE**

Hexagonal designs are everywhere in nature—petals of a flower, snowflakes, and in the chambers of a honeycomb! This tiny book makes a lovely table decoration for garden-themed soirees, party favors, or thank-you gifts.

YOU WILL NEED

Watercolor paper for text block

Matte board

Decorative paper for covers

Decorative paper for end papers

Silk ribbon

Beads

Glue

Scoring tool

Craft knife

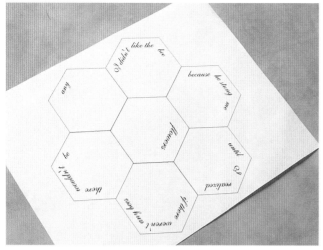

1 Trace the template (see page 77), using a ruler for straight lines, and cut the entire shape out of the water color paper. You may draw or write your design on now, if you wish. If you are using words, arrange your writing following their position on the template.

2 Score all the fold lines on the hexagonal page.

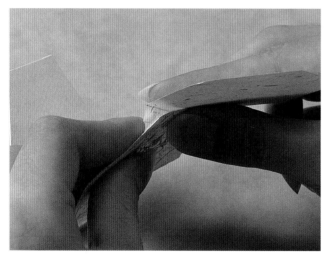

3 Cut out your end paper by using one hexagon of the template as the example, but add an extra ¼ inch (1 cm) to one of the ends. This will create a tab. Fold the tab back and apply glue there, as well as to the back of the center hexagon, and press together. Set aside.

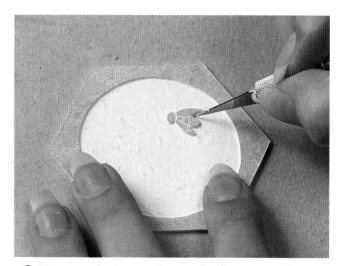

4 To create the impression on the front cover, draw a bee somewhere in the center of one cover board (which is also cut in the same hexagon shape). Draw a circle within the edges of the hexagon and carve out the inside layers with a craft knife. Once the circle is cut, it will be easier to peel away the layers. Be sure to leave the bee area intact, then carve around this in more detail.

VARIATION

You may enlarge or reduce the pattern to your liking. Based on the size of your pattern, measure your cover boards and end papers. Cover board may be ⅛ inch (3 mm) larger than the text page which will be glued to it.

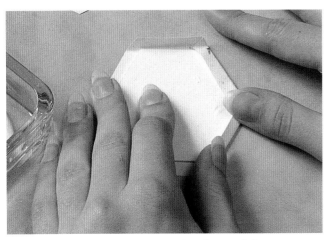

5 Apply glue thinly to one side of one of the cover boards. Center the cover board, glue side down, over the cover paper. Apply glue to the edges of the cover paper. Fold each of the six sides of the paper around the cover board. Crease it firmly around the board.

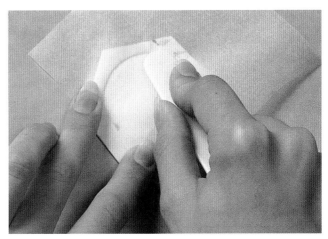

6 Smooth the paper over the front of the board. For the cover with the bee, place a piece of thin paper over the covered board, and using your scoring tool, smooth the paper around and over the bee and into the circular groove framing the cover, so that the bee and frame have definition.

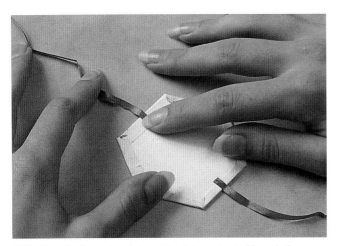

7 Cut the length of the silk ribbon in half and glue each piece to opposite sides of the back inside cover.

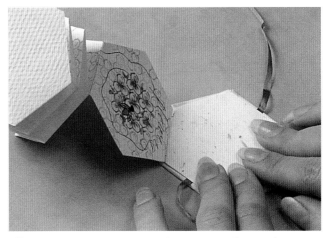

8 Fold the text paper you have cut and scored. Start with the first fold at "page 1," then continue around the hexagon, ending with the end paper lying against the back of the book. Apply glue to the wrong side of the top of the folded book. Insert scrap paper under the top page to protect the book. Make sure cover is right side up, with top and bottom matched with top and bottom of folded book. Press the cover board down. Flip the book over and repeat with the other board.

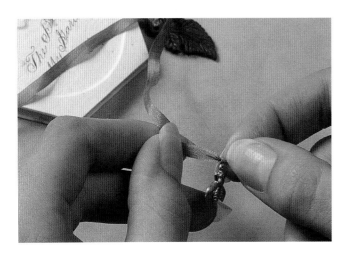

9 Tie charms or beads on ribbons and tie in a bow.

Pattern for Hexagonal Bee Book, page 73
Enlarge or reduce as desired

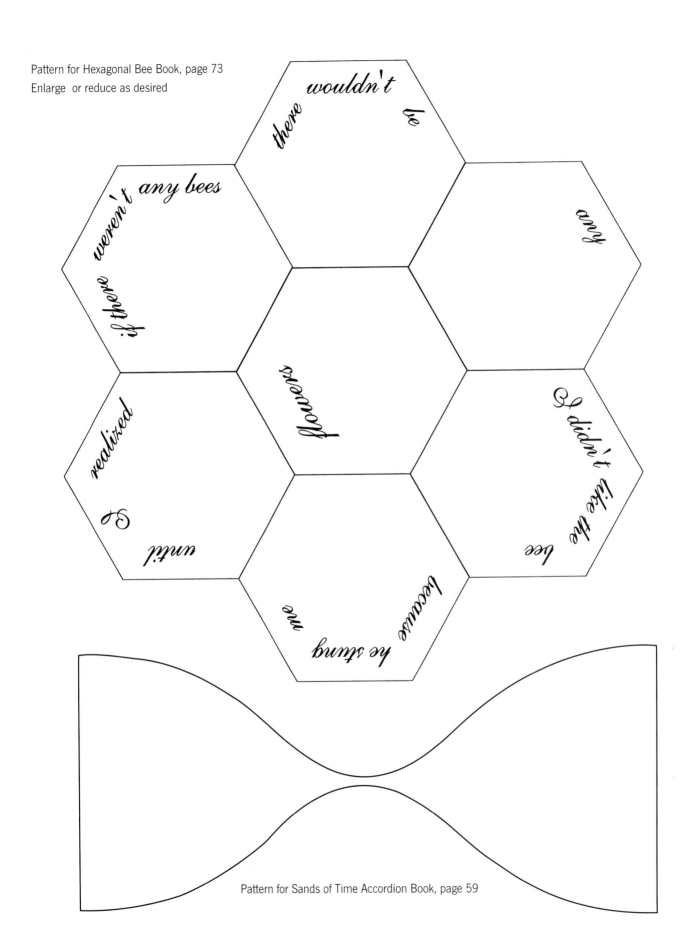

Pattern for Sands of Time Accordion Book, page 59

Pattern for Shell Book, page 70
Enlarge 125%

Pattern for Angel Photo Album, page 28

GLOSSARY

Here are the bookbinding and book-making terms we use in our book, as well as some you will undoubtedly encounter if you continue your bookmaking adventures.

ACCORDION FOLD: a piece, or several pasted pieces, of paper folded front to back, in a zig-zag, or Chinese fan pattern

ADHESIVES: any kind of glue or paste used to bond the bookbinding materials together

ARTIST'S BOOK: usually a one-of-a-kind book created by an artist for exhibition purposes

AWL: a tool with a handle for gripping and a sharp, pointed end for creating holes in paper and boards; in order to accommodate thread for sewing the pieces of the book together

BINDER'S BOARD (MATTE BOARD): any stiff board material used by bookmakers as the covers of books

BONE FOLDER: a flat tool made of animal bone, with thin rounded edges and a blunt point, for creasing paper and flattening book edges and corners

BURNISHING: flattening a surface (usually paper glued over board) with a blunt-edged tool, to rid the surface of air bubbles, creases, and any other imperfections in the texture; burnishing can also smooth the texture of paper and produce a subtle shine on the paper surface

CODEX: early definition of a manuscript or book; a bundle of text pages between two boards

COLOPHONE: an inscription at the end of a book, listing specifics as to its production

CONCERTINA: another name for accordion fold

COPTIC BINDING: the earliest known binding of the codex format; sewn together with a chain stitch

COVER PAPER: any paper used to cover the boards which house text pages

DECKLE EDGES: the rough edges of handmade paper formed in a deckle; also, edges which have been cut with special scissors, creating a design along the edges, rather than a smooth and even edge

DOS-À-DOS BINDING: two books bound back to back which open in opposite directions and share one board

ENDPAPERS: decorative papers which cover the inside of the cover boards of a book

FOLIO: a set of four pages produced when folding one page into four equal sections

HINGE: the space between the the cover board and a thin strip of the board, bound together with a thinner material to ease opening the cover

LOTUS BOOK: a book which is square when closed, but opens out like a flower when the inner edges are pulled out, resulting in a larger square when laid flat

SCORING: creasing a piece of paper evenly with a bone-folder or other blunt-edged tool, to ensure smooth opening and closing

SIGNATURE: sections of text pages placed together, one inside the other, generally for sewing and placing between book covers

SPINE: the edge of a book, where the text pages and book covers come together

CONTRIBUTING DESIGNERS

DORIS ARNDT has been a freelance artist for over 20 years and has been published in a variety of magazines. She lives in Tacoma, WA and teaches paper arts throughout the U.S.

JOYCE BRODSKY is a mixed-media artist whose recent works have focused on bookarts, fiber, and surface design. In recent work she has been involved with calligraphy, hand papermaking and soft sculpture. Working with mixed media affords her the wide array of materials to combine color and textures which serve as inspiration.

KRISTIN COZZOLINO received her BFA in printmaking from the University of the Arts in Philadelphia. Originally from Rhode Island, she now lives in Asheville, NC, specializing in hanging sculptures made with kozo fiber and other natural materials.

ELLEN DAUGHERTY is a first-grade teacher in Williamston, MI.

GWEN DIEHN teaches art and art education at Warren Wilson College near Asheville, NC. She has exhibited her drawings, prints, and artist books nationally. She is the author of several books for children: Nature Crafts for Kids, (Sterling/Lark, 1992); Science Crafts for Kids (Sterling/Lark 1994); Kid Style Nature Crafts (Sterling/Lark, 1995); Making Books that Fly, Fold, Wrap, Hide, Pop-up, Twist and Turn (Lark Books, 1998).

STEPHANIE ELLIS has a Bachelor of Fine Arts degree from the University of North Carolina–Charlotte. She now lives in Asheville, NC, painting and making handmade paper, journals, and books.

CONTRIBUTING DESIGNERS

DAISY KAPPEN lives in Valencia, CA. She designs stickers, clip-art books, stationery, greeting cards, business logos, and gift items. Access her web page at the following address: http://freeyellow.com/members/dreamimpressions.

PAULA BEARDELL KRIEG is an artist, teaching bookmaking and paper decorating skills, extensively in the Northeast. She also makes books with her two small children, John and Angela, in upstate New York.

JULIA MONROE made her first book, a tiny 1-inch-high, four-signature activity book of dot-to-dots, crossword puzzles and coloring pages, when she was 11 years old. Years later she taught herself how to make a "proper" hard-cover book. Of all the arts and crafts she does, bookbinding is her favorite. She has taught several classes on bookbinding. She lives in North Carolina with her husband and their six children.

NICOLE TUGGLE combines bookbinding techniques with her passion for mail art to create unique letters and gift items. She uses her art as a means of communication, emotional release, and to celebrate the simple act of giving.

BETH WEISS is a book artist and calligrapher always seeking unusual materials and forms for her one-of-a-kind pieces. Her work is exhibited nationally and appears in corporate and private collections. She studied music and art in college and has gone on to train with some of the foremost calligraphers and book artists in the country. Once Beth has acquired a new technique or skill, she is anxious to share it with students to see where they take it in their own work.

A NOTE ABOUT SUPPLIERS

Usually, the supplies you need for making the projects in Lark books can be found at your local craft supply store, discount mart, home improvement center, or retail shop relevant to the topic of the book. Occasionally, however, you may need to buy materials or tools from specialty suppliers. In order to provide you with the most up-to-date information, we have created a listing of suppliers on our Website, which we update on a regular basis. Visit us at www.larkbooks.com, click on "Craft Supply Sources," and then click on the relevant topic. You will find numerous companies listed with their web address and/or mailing address and phone number.

ACKNOWLEDGMENTS

Special thanks to consultant Gwen Diehn for sharing her expertise and insight as an accomplished artist, bookmaking instructor, and writer, and for contributing her own eclectic projects.

Thank you to Deborah Morganthal for her patience and assistance with all questions asked, and for the chance to create this book. Thanks to photographer Evan Bracken, who makes magic, and is never without a sense of humor; and to art director Celia Naranjo, who beautifully dressed these books and created sense out of less-than-sensible files. A big thank you to Nicole Tuggle for the photographic use of her long, tapered fingers and artistic hands, as well as for her lovely book contributions.

A special thanks to Julia Monroe, who tirelessly created a bounty of extraordinary, unique projects for this book and who is an inspiration with her hard work and enthusiasm.

Thank you, also, to True Blue Art Supply & Services, Inc. for the use of their materials, Coral and Heather made picking out paper a joy.

And last, but not least, thank you to all the phenomenal designers who contributed to this book—they are masters of patience as well as their art

INDEX